CHRIST THE RECONCILER

Christ the Reconciler

A Theology for Opposites, Differences, and Enemies

Peter Schmiechen

WILLIAM B. EERDMANS PUBLISHING COMPANY
GRAND RAPIDS, MICHIGAN / CAMBRIDGE, U.K.

© 1996 Wm. B. Eerdmans Publishing Co.
255 Jefferson Ave. S.E., Grand Rapids, Michigan 49503 /
P.O. Box 163, Cambridge CB3 9PU U.K.

Printed in the United States of America

01 00 99 98 97 96   7 6 5 4 3 2 1

ISBN 0-8028-4178-3

To
Will
Alexandra and Zoe

Contents

Preface

This essay has grown from two sources: one is the conviction that the life and work of the church should be governed by our primary affirmations of faith; the other is the many years of conversation with pastors and students regarding the present crisis in the church. The former has always driven me back to theology; the latter has forced me to consider how we can envision a future beyond the present crisis. Given the radical polarization and conflict within the church, surrounded by a violent world, I have found pastors weighed down with the burdens of ministry. The prospect of moving beyond division and conflict, of a recovery of confidence regarding the church's proclamation, of a word of grace rather than judgment — such a prospect has brought excitement and hope to conversations. It is my conviction that we shall not move beyond the present crisis without hearing again the word of the cross as both judgment and promise, for the church as well as the world.

In the summer of 1994 I was asked to speak at a conference on the crisis of the church. Having submitted a rather standard title, the director asked me to consider a more imaginative title. After reflection I suggested: "The Church: Why It's

Broke and Why We Can't Fix It!" Much to my surprise the title aroused interest as well as multiplied attendance. That experience did more than demonstrate the power of language. It convinced me that we must offer the most radically honest analysis of our present situation, but also point beyond the analysis to the gospel of reconciliation.

This book therefore operates on several levels. It involves an analysis of our situation in American culture as well as the internal struggles within Protestant churches. Over against such analysis the book constructs a social theory of atonement, which is then used to reconstruct our view of the nature and mission of the church. There is no doubt that such an approach moves in radically different directions. I find it necessary to connect such diverse elements because they are key issues in the present crisis.

Along the way, my colleagues at Lancaster Theological Seminary have patiently listened and offered constructive comments. Lee Barrett, Anabel Proffitt, Frank Stalfa, and David Greenhaw have been part of a lively conversation. I also wish to thank the Trustees of the Seminary for granting a sabbatical leave of absence in the fall of 1994, which allowed me to complete the project. For their support and encouragement I am indeed grateful. A word of thanks must also be given to Rev. William Fossum and the members of Grace Lutheran Church in Ely, Minnesota, for allowing me to use a quiet space in their church for writing during the summer of 1994. Ms. Mary Lin Siever has assisted me in the preparation of the manuscript, and I am grateful to her for her excellent work.

PETER SCHMIECHEN

Introduction

This essay is a call for theological reform of the church. By this we do not mean a scholastic review of the church's faith, with a prescription to return to standard doctrines. Such an approach would be ineffective, though not because of any fault in the creeds. They are indeed the rule of faith. The fault lies in the state of American churches, which are so divided internally that a call to return to a particular creedal platform would only further divide. By theological we mean the recovery of the gospel as a vision for the life of the church and its proclamation to the world. The basic issue facing ecumenical Protestantism is not the so-called collapse of the mainline or the threat of secularism, but the inability to see the gospel as the liberating and reconciling power of God. Protestant churches have become in effect dysfunctional: divided into competing parts, they have allowed the culture to dictate the shape and substance of religion. Unable to represent the peace of Christ in their own life, they are unable to proclaim it to the world.

Theological reform is to be distinguished from several other approaches to reform. The first is moral reform. There have always been calls for the moral reform of the church's life and action. In the social revolutions of the '60s and '70s, the church was rebuked for its inability to join the great movements for social change. These critiques included resounding calls to action. But such attempts at reform were ineffective because engagement in social/political life was not part of the agreement when most of the members had joined the church. They understood the being and doing of the church in highly individualistic terms. Thus, when criticized, they never felt guilty. In fact, they were outraged that religious leaders were involved in these social revolutions — they could not even comprehend it! A call to action has difficulty going beyond the enthusiasm of the particular crisis unless people can connect the call to their understanding of the gospel. Moral reform must be grounded in an authentic faith, nurtured by the grace and justice of God.

A second group of reformers sees major changes in the relations between the church and the world to be the decisive factor. In the last forty years there has been a steady stream of analysis regarding the loss of Protestant supremacy, new forms of disestablishment, the decline of the mainline in numbers and influence, and the rise of secularism. From Harvey Cox's *The Secular City* to Loren Mead's *Once and Future Church,* shifts in the church-world relation are taken to be the starting point for reform. These perspectives tend to ignore the enduring character of religion and the fact that in America religion always changes. Churches in America have displayed a capacity for adapting and surviving in the face of the most radical shifts in the culture. Moreover, the arguments regarding secularity and disestablishment tend to look to trends in Europe rather than America. In America the vast majority of the people are religious. The problem is not lack of faith but the substance of faith and competing faiths. Americans look to the churches for moral leadership and a vision for society.

A method closer to theological reform is doctrinal reform.

What distinguishes this approach is not its goal of a community joining in confession of the catholic faith. Rather, it is differentiated by its insistence that doctrine itself can be the means of renewal. It proposes to reform the church by means of a return to creeds and confessions, and even the writing of a new catechism. In effect, it assumes that we can call people to come home to the ancestral confessions and thereby restore the unity and vitality of the church.

Doctrinal reform fails to see the radical pluralism and division present in the church. Such pluralism prohibits a rallying around any one doctrinal tradition, either because it never was everyone's common tradition or because many people tie such a tradition to negative experiences. The fact is that most Christians do not link their faith to creeds and doctrines, nor do they have overwhelmingly positive remembrances of doctrinal instruction. In a more general way, doctrinal reform fails to see that true religion is not doctrine, which is secondary and derived from the primary expressions of faith. Christianity consists, in the primary sense, in the reality of the new life Jesus Christ creates in the community of faith and the world. It finds expression in acts of faith, hope, and love. It is instructed by confessions and doctrines but cannot be equated with them. Faith and its formal confessions witness to Jesus Christ, the Lord and Savior present in the world. Faith is a gift of the Spirit, nurtured by evangelical preaching and sacramental grace.

At the present time, doctrinal reform is usually driven by the conviction that the church is cut off from its true life, a separation illustrated by erroneous views and the excesses of individualism. In virtually every ecumenical church there are movements to return to the certainty of orthodox faith. Such movements rightly see the problem as one of theological substance, rather than strategy, but their solutions are too often scholastic and reactive. In some cases they are fundamentalistic in nature. By calling the church back to the correctness of an earlier time, they tend to superimpose on the present, with its particular people and needs, the formulae from another generation. In their tendency to set boundaries, they appear authoritarian and exclusive, thereby turning attention on themselves as a point of controversy. What is lost in such scholasticism is the encounter of the gospel with the church today in ways that will liberate and renew its faith and life for our time.[1]

Finally, theological reform can be distinguished from a fourth approach, which is basically strategic. Here the problem facing churches is understood as the loss of mission; the solution is therefore designed to enable churches to reorganize and focus

---

1. Loren Mead's analysis of our situation is so dominated by the loss of Christendom that one cannot help but feel the subject is the decline of state churches in England and northern Europe. To be sure, the old Protestant mainline in America has fallen on hard times, but not because the Constantinian establishment has come to an end. A more close-at-hand analysis is needed, as well as a greater appreciation for the changes effected by reforms in the sixteenth and eighteenth centuries. For example, in America disestablishment occurred over two hundred years ago, and we have gone through several major revisions of the church-society relation. In Mead's essay there is little appreciation for the genius of the American formula for church-state relations: no state church exists, but religion is a major force in the society. The relation of religion to the society has gone through major changes, and we are living through one now. Nevertheless, these changes are probably not understood by comparing them to Protestant Europe. A new mainline may already have emerged, if we are willing to recognize it. It is not the so-called conservative majority, but an ecumenical one. If, for example, one adds up the membership of liberal and moderate Protestants and adds a major portion of Catholics and Jews, one has over 50 percent of the American population. The old Protestant mainline has been replaced by a new mainline of ecumenically minded Protestants, Catholics, and Jews. The question therefore is, are we willing to play with the new players, or will we sit in the bleachers and grieve? For membership data, see Wade Clark Roof and William McKinney, *American Mainline Religion: Its Changing Shape and Future* (New Brunswick: Rutgers University Press, 1987), 82. See also Loren Mead, *The Once and Future Church: Reinventing the Congregation for a New Mission Frontier* (Washington: Publications Program of the Alban Institute, 1991).

on mission in the world. Thirty years ago this approach produced calls for the church to leave the comfort of suburbia and middle-class isolation. In our time Loren Mead advocates a redefinition of mission and the empowerment of the laity, while Kennon Callahan identifies mission to nonmembers as the key for vitality and growth.[2] One can hardly quarrel with a call to mission. The problem, however, is that such approaches tend to leave untouched the way so much of Protestantism is dysfunctional with respect to its theology and organization. There can be no enthusiasm and recommitment to mission unless there is a new vision of the gospel for our time that opens up a new understanding of what God is doing in the world. Too often mission is proposed as a strategy based on duty (i.e., it is something we ought to do); in its worst form it is proposed as a technique that will revive dying churches (i.e., get new members and raise more money).[3] But you can not add mission — be it evangelism or social service — to churches constructed on the basis of individualistic piety and consumer religion.

For example, consider the challenge ecumenical Protestants face in evangelism. American culture assigns the highest value to the freedom of the individual. From this starting point, it locates religion in the private realm of individual free choice. Just as people should have the right to choose their husband or wife, a career, or a place to live, so they have an inviolable right to choose a religion — or no religion at all. But how free individuals act toward other persons and what they do in

2. Cf. Mead, chs. IV, V, and VI, pp. 43ff., and Kennon L. Callahan, *Twelve Keys to an Effective Church: Strategic Planning for Mission* (San Francisco: Harper, 1983), ix-xxxi and 1-9.

3. This reference to the abuse of mission refers to general practice and not to either Loren Mead or Kennon Callahan. In general, Callahan's perspective is marked by a sound and rich theological framework that avoids the reduction of strategic planning for the church to techniques designed to get results at all costs.

society constitute the public side of life. If someone pollutes the earth and endangers the health of others, one has a right to intervene: to ask that a person cease such activity and, if possible, restore the earth. If a person starves his/her children, one has a right to intervene in the name of the physical safety of the children. But does one have a right to tell someone what to believe, if belief falls into the sacred, private domain of individual freedom? In effect, we are quite confident that we may intervene in matters of public safety, but not at all so sure that we can intervene in matters of faith. How then do Protestants, so tied to a culture of freedom, practice evangelism? To ask someone about the state of their soul is an intrusion into someone's inner life. It is both an impoliteness and a violation of freedom. Is it any wonder that the mainline churches are caught with a decline in numbers when growth by other means comes to an end? How then do they now reorganize for evangelism, without acknowledging the contradictions inherent in the religion of American culture? Such a dilemma, born of the loss of vision and will, points to the need for theological reform.

This essay begins with an examination of the religious situation: the shape and substance of American religion (Chapter One); the divisions within the churches over the nature and mission of the church (Chapter Two); and the way contemporary culture causes persons to define themselves in terms that challenge Christian faith (Chapter Three). In Chapter Four we turn to an interpretation of the cross and resurrection of Jesus Christ as a means to uncover the power of the gospel. Consistent with the concept of theological reform, Chapter Five reconstructs a view of the church (its nature, proclamation, and action) on the Christological affirmations rooted in the gospel of reconciliation. Such an ordering of things affirms that the doing of the church must grow out of its being, and that its being will possess reconciling power only if it is grounded in the new life God gives to the world.

CHAPTER 1

The American Inheritance

Things do not always turn out as planned. The old epic history tells of religious groups coming to America for freedom and toleration. In actuality most came to create theocratic communities where they could have it their way. To some extent this was inevitable, since once separatists got here, they had no state from which to separate. Each group, regardless of its intention, found it possible and necessary to participate in the shaping of new societies. But in the end the churches were shaped by America in ways never expected. The American formation of Christianity is still taking place, offering opportunities and limits, but relentlessly demanding that churches deal with changes generated by forces unique to this land.

We begin by examining two ways that the American experience has formed religious faith and life. One is the primacy of the individual; the other is the triumph of doing over being. By the former I mean that American religion is founded on the freedom of the individual to believe and do whatever a person chooses. By the latter I mean that American religion is practical and functional: It exists to do something and is justified only if it does something. When the two are joined together, religion must do something for me! These two principles of American religion account for much of its creativity and strength, as well as its problems and weaknesses. Nowhere in the world do churches look more lively, powerful, and active, but nowhere are they more divided and concerned about the future.

The story of a religious mind-set so dependent on individualism and functionalism is directly tied to the story of the nation itself. This development tells us much about our contemporary situation, since we live within the structural limits of that social history. Unfortunately, our religious history in America tends to be neglected. In our deference to tradition we look to Europe for explanations and trends. Yet few American churches look or act like their European parents. The most significant factors forming the churches are here, imbedded in our own history. In this case the story may in fact be written in stone, and it may take a Joshua to break down the walls that control us.

The American movement for independence reflected both traditional religious ideas and the current liberal/rational social views of the Enlightenment. The most fundamental starting point was the individual. In John Locke, rational and free individuals create social order by consenting to give up personal freedom for the sake of the common good. When applied to the idea of a new democracy, this meant that the new nation consisted of individuals and the states they themselves had created, banding together to create a nation. Government was founded on religious principles, but these were not sanctioned by a church or churches. They were themselves self-evident and universal, accessible to human reason in the Book of Nature. The new social order consisted of individuals endowed by their Creator with rights, the chief being life, liberty, and the pursuit of happiness.

This concept of the state was radically new and an experiment of great risk. On the one hand it required a separation of church and state, with each side granting to the other free-dom and authority based on a transcendent authority. On the other hand, it required a moral and religious life that would undergird the social order, based not on a state church but on voluntary acceptance by members of the society. No one ever argued that you could have a new nation without moral and religious beliefs; what they advocated was the free expression and cultivation of such as a means to support the public good. If then the new political order consisted of individuals banding together to create a government, the newly disestablished churches were defined as individuals banding together to create religious communities. The origin of this theory has been chronicled in many places, most recently in Bellah's *The Good Society*.[1] Its consequences on social and religious institutions are far-reaching and devastating. Here let us consider its impact by charting the formative power of individualism and function-alism.

The Shape of American Religion: Individualism

America is fundamentally a set of values that constitute a vision of a new social order. At the heart of these ideas is liberty. Indeed, one can argue that if forced to choose between liberty and community, freedom and justice, most Americans will choose liberty. It is the essential thing that binds us together. In part this is because we are not bound by blood, religion,

---

1. Robert N. Bellah et al., *The Good Society* (New York: Alfred A. Knopf, 1991). Compare also Robert N. Bellah et al., *Habits of the Heart: Individualism and Commitment in American Life* (Berkeley: University of California Press, 1985); Wade Clark Roof and William McKinney, *American Mainline Religion: Its Changing Shape and Future* (New Brunswick: Rutgers University Press, 1987); and the classic work by Sidney E. Mead, *The Lively Experiment: The Shaping of Christianity in America* (New York: Harper and Row, 1963).

tradition, class, or region. But in positive terms, freedom is the tie that binds because one must choose to be an American. There is, of course, a circle here: in freedom we choose freedom. It can be no other way. A free society assumes that its members will voluntarily pledge allegiance to its most essential values.

The agent of this freedom is the individual. It is in this sense that America means the primacy of the individual and the individual's right to liberty. In the ideal, each person is to be a free, rational, informed citizen participating in the work of society for the common good. Everyone knows that this is not always the case. But since most attempts to require people to do the good have been oppressive, a free society tends to choose freedom even if it means the possibility of bad choices and/or self-destructive behavior.[2] It is not against the law to waste your money, make bad investments, overeat, smoke, or consume too much alcohol. In a free society, not only is the individual primary, but so is free choice. Free choice (i.e., autonomy) is thus elevated to a higher status than other values, making the individual responsible for a wide range of decisions and activities. Since religion is one of the activities that falls under the domain of individual freedom, religion so practiced will have the following characteristics.

1. Religion is a matter of personal choice. One chooses to be or not to be religious. One also chooses how one will be religious. It is not part of one's citizenship, nor a legal requirement for employment or social status. Given the plurality of religious traditions, it could be no other way. The move to disestablishment was as much a defensive measure to prevent

---

2. This preference for freedom is best defended by the classic work of John Stuart Mill, *On Liberty*, whose language now permeates the liberal tradition. The problem, however, is whether Mill's standard for liberty (namely, no harm to another person) is practical or effective in a mass, technological society, where the traditional constraints on excessive freedom are all but removed.

others from becoming the state church as it was a genuine affirmation of toleration. But to say religion is personal involves a uniquely American paradox: Though personal, it has always been assumed to have many positive relations to the public good. Personal has not always meant private. For the most part the religious traditions have shared a general public faith that, while never a state church, supported and proclaimed a higher purpose and a set of values.[3] This public faith has coexisted with the institutions of government, and, in general, the two have interacted in positive ways. The genius of the American experiment, which is still being tested and worked out, is that it holds together separation of the government from religious institutions with minimal limitation on the opportunity for believers to influence and shape the public good. While religion is a personal choice, such choices can affect the society when translated into the language of social, political, or economic values.

That religion is something people choose accounts in part for the tremendous vitality and creativity of religion in America. A multitude of traditions have been sustained by the voluntary sacrifice and commitment of members. New movements have been born and old institutions have been reformed in order to deal with changing needs. But religion founded on personal choice is also open to peculiar challenges and even temptations. Three come quickly to mind, and we might call them the three great American heresies. The most obvious is that while most Americans acknowledge belief in God, far fewer are active in churches or synagogues. Thus the first great American heresy: one can be religious and not go to church! Such a practice flows naturally from the autonomy of the individual. It leads to the second heresy: in a free society the individual is free not

3. Cf. Robert N. Bellah, "Civil Religion in America," *Daedalus: Journal of the American Academy of Arts and Sciences* 96 (Winter 1967): 1-21.

only from the state, but also from tradition, family, ecclesial authority, and sacred texts. One can in effect, "Believe anything you want." The third American heresy violates both the religious heritage and the spirit of the American experiment: it is to confine religion to the privacy of an individual spiritual life. In our century this is seen as a natural consequence of the personal nature of religion. On the one hand this means the confinement of religion to the realm of the personal, which has come to mean the subjective, as the antithesis of the real, objective world. On the other hand it opens the way for the creation of a secular, value-free public life based on technological and utilitarian goals. Such a worldview sees religion as irrelevant and even a source of social division, since religious people do not agree.[4]

The redefinition of religion as private and subjective prompts some to give up religion completely and others to practice a worldly religion that shuns spirituality, lest one be drawn away from the real world. One of the casualties of this dichotomy of private spirituality versus public faith has been the word *personal*. When conservative evangelists admonish their listeners: "You must have a personal relation with Jesus!" it usually evokes a negative reaction from liberal Protestants. They assume that the word *personal* is code language for private, individualized religion removed from public witness or service. Hence they are repelled by the word. So deep is the reaction that many liberals have tried to sustain the Christian life without the practice of personal piety. The recovery of spirituality in the last decade among ecumenical, liberal Protestants has been in part a move toward overcoming the dichotomy of personal spirituality and public witness. But the damage has been done to the word *personal*, and the issue is not entirely resolved.

4. Cf. Stephen L. Carter, *The Culture of Disbelief: How American Law and Politics Trivialize Religious Devotion* (New York: Basic Books, 1993), 1-66.

2. If religion is a personal decision by free individuals, then they must be persuaded. "Almost Persuaded" may be a gospel song known primarily by revivalistic churches, but sooner or later all churches discover that they must be active in recruiting members. Persuasion and recruitment inevitably follow from religious freedom. A long history of awakenings, camp meetings, revivals, and new measures in every generation, leading to radio and television evangelism, has established the pattern. Evangelism has always been the process of telling the story of God's mighty acts. But in America it must also focus on persuading individuals to choose Christ and the church.

In the past twenty years the old mainline, ecumenical denominations have experienced major losses in membership, often in the 20 to 30 percent range. Coupled with the rise in the influence of Roman Catholics and conservative Protestants, there has been a great debate over the decline of these denominations. Countless explanations have been given, pointing to greater secularity or a shift in public attitudes to conservatism. A simpler explanation is readily at hand in the shape of American religion: these denominations have not attended to the persuasion of free individuals. It is even more embarrassing: Roof and McKinney argue that the decline has been mainly in the loss of our children.[5] In the past twenty years the children of mainline churches left, apparently because attending church did not make any difference. The mainline churches assumed they had a steady stream of new members by birth and natural attraction. As I will argue later, many of these churches by default did not attend to evangelism, education, fund raising, or new church building. Now it is time to face this omission. But to do so when Protestantism is not the socially established religion means we must come to terms with the voluntarism of American religious life.

5. Roof and McKinney, 11-39.

The requirement for persuasion brings with it obvious temptations. The focus on persuasion of free individuals produces a religious world where the individual is in control. A religious consumerism is created where the church asks, "What do they want?" and the potential member asks, "What will you do for me?" This self-centeredness has been the negative side of free religion throughout our history. It holds the potential of changing the gospel from a call to hear God's will to an appeal to the listener's needs and interests. As early as the Great Awakening, religious persuasion discovered that the outcome could be affected by the means used. Once people began to think about this, all manner of techniques were developed to assure the right outcome. Certain styles of preaching, types of music, themes, lighting, and settings could all be used to achieve the desired result. If persuasion is the key, then *method* becomes as important as *substance*. The distortions are everywhere. We may be able to overcome these distortions, but we will not eliminate the temptation, given the crucial role of persuasion in American religion.

3. In a free society, where there is no state church, religious communities must be redefined. The American answer has been to locate churches on a social/political map in the realm of voluntary associations. The church is a gathering of people, united and legally incorporated, for a specific purpose. Individuals choose to enter, remain, or leave according to their needs and interests. As an association of members, the church may grow or decline, live or die.

This shape of the church brings with it two unfortunate consequences. One is the assumption, sometimes never stated but often celebrated, that the church has no reality except for what is bestowed on it by the believers. In effect, the church is not grounded in objective realities outside the self (e.g., the Body of Christ), but now finds its foundation in the will of the members. In such a church, language about the sovereignty of

God, a divine will, authority of the Bible, or the authority of the ordained ministry will be difficult to sustain. To be sure, there will be much talk about God and the Bible, but understood according to the special interests of the believers. After all, the church is now an association of believers.

A second consequence is that the basis of union for the association lies within the members who created it. It is a voluntary association of *like-minded people.* (In most cases, it is also an association of the same color, class, national origin, and social attitudes.) The strength of the church now passes from Jesus as Lord and Savior to the members. The strength of the community is defined in terms of the sum of the commitment of the members to one another. Most church growth strategy assumes you must seek out like-minded people, who will fit in and find their needs met because they are like the members. Such a view of the church perpetuates the isolation of people, since churches will seldom cross the lines of division in our society. But just as important, what will happen when this association of believers discovers that it is not like-minded? What will hold them together? Who will pay the price for such division when there are no objective norms to hold them together? No wonder the past three decades have been tough on clergy.

4. Related to all of these characteristics is the dominance of social-political language to define the church. The American experiment has imposed on the church a language that replaces the theological language of its origin. When religion is defined as a voluntary association, it is appropriate and even necessary to speak of autonomy, association, and mutual obligations. Parliamentary procedure, with its either/or, win/lose alternatives, provides the accepted process. The Christian language, so rich in images of divine sovereignty, grace and forgiveness, prayer and reconciliation, is radically altered. This change in language also changes the church.

15

To illustrate this change, we can track the change in meaning of the word *covenant* in the Free Church tradition coming from England. The Free Church movement arose out of rebellion against the tyranny of a state church. Kings and bishops opposed the free expression of the gospel and tried to prevent new leadings of the Spirit. This produced a break with the state church in the name of the freedom of the individual and the congregation. But for seventeenth- and eighteenth-century Congregationalists who came to the new world, this freedom was qualified by traditional theological images. The language of covenant still had substantive theological value. Since it was the covenant of Jesus Christ, the fellowship was also Christ's and not one that we create. To be sure, it was a community that one must enter freely, but it was a real community that existed outside the individual as a reality in its own right. It was divinely constituted and had objective standards: Bible, creed, and a history of covenants.

By the middle of the nineteenth century a radical shift had occurred. The United States Constitution required the disestablishment of regional state churches, which were now defined as voluntary associations. The freedom of the individual was primary; religion was a matter of personal choice. *Covenant* now comes to mean an association human beings create, sustain, manage, and even dissolve. Such covenants grow out of human autonomy and must be restricted so as not to limit individual or group autonomy. The dialectic between God and humanity, the individual and the community, freedom and order, has been shattered. We are left with an organizational system where the parts are separate units, held together by personal agreements and admonitions. Community has been broken because the context of covenantal language is no longer a divinely constituted community where Christ is head, but a human construction with a social-political context, where autonomous individuals negotiate rights and obligations.

This shift in the meaning of a biblical word, so rich in theological meaning, creates a serious problem for interpreting its use. When it is used to describe the relation between members or to appeal for certain action, does that use refer to a reality that transcends the individual and provides the necessary context for individual existence? Does it refer to judgment and grace that are objectively given whether the individual acknowledges or rejects them? Above all, does it refer to that new reality that God creates according to Jesus Christ? Or does it refer to a social-political association arising out of the members, which they sustain by agreement and control by their action? The domination of individualism as the shape of American religion makes it highly probable that the latter meaning is intended.

We have reviewed the impact of individualism and its many consequences for the faith and life of the church: the autonomous individual, the persuasion that creates religious consumerism, the church redefined as a voluntary association humans create and control, and, finally, the loss of a theological vocabulary. These are systemic, structural issues, dealing with the very substance of Christian existence. They have affected American Christianity in a most radical way. When a Lutheran pastor was asked how he found ministry in a church where people still knew something of a tradition and ethos, he responded: "No, they all act like Baptists." What he meant was that even in his Lutheran congregation, the dominant mind-set is that of the individual forging the religious life all by oneself. This is the end product of the American experiment. It is not enough to be against individualism, or issue a new call to mission, or attempt charismatic preaching. We need to reform the very structure of American religion from a theological point of view.

The Substance of American Religion:
Functionalism

A culture that takes as its starting point the primacy of the individual and assigns freedom the highest value will have a low view of institutions and community. Robert Bellah and his colleagues have laid out the philosophical and cultural origins of this view.[6] If the free, rational self is posited as primary, then individuals create institutions only out of practical necessity to perform functions. They are utilitarian in nature. Moreover, this perspective includes a high degree of skepticism and caution regarding institutions. Tradition and hierarchical authority, as lodged in institutions, are the major threats to individual freedom. Given the abuses of power, the American tradition has a built-in fear and even hatred of institutions. But since individuals must endure or tolerate them, they must be functional: the sole purpose of communal structures and offices is to do something. It is the triumph of doing over being, of means over ends.

Within the church this antipathy toward institutions takes the form of a disregard for the things that nurture, sustain, and build up a common life. Simply put, the liberal church has such a weak ecclesiology because it is incapable of a positive view of community. The fear of institutionalism and the repressive side of institutions so dominates the liberal mind-set that it is unable to see the void. In a sense we know something is missing, but we are unable to articulate the unmet need because of our fear. This situation creates an ambivalence toward structure, power, authority, and the maintenance of institutions. On the one hand we talk about them in order to overcome repression and enhance liberty. But we also fear them because they are the stuff of institutional life. This in part explains why so

6. Bellah, *Good Society*, 1-110.

many mainline churches don't know what to do with evangelism and stewardship: to ask people to join or give you have to believe in the church.

It is currently quite popular to chastise the rationalism of the seventeenth and eighteenth centuries. But why is it that functionalism was so well received and easily assimilated into American religious life? Functionalism has become a virtual article of faith for Protestants, but not by accident. If Protestantism did not inspire it — and it may have — then it certainly has supported it. We must look, therefore, at the ways basic religious ideas have been used and abused to support functionalism. Likewise, the alternative to functionalism will require more than criticism of John Locke; it will require an honest revision of the way several key Protestant themes have been understood.

Two themes central to the Reformation have been used to support functionalism. The first deals with ordained offices. Let us remember that Protestantism was a reform of the church, as well as a theological reform. Among its many practical reforms, it objected to the distinction between the religious orders and the laity as two levels of the religious life. The medieval world had created a hierarchy of religious orders over the laity, entailing distinctions of value. The church and its offices existed to perform duties, but also claimed substantive value as ends in themselves. Hierarchy was only one consequence of the dividing of religious and lay.

By contrast, Protestantism started with the equality of all believers by virtue of their baptismal calling. It declared that offices in the church were secondary to this sacrament and denied that ordination was even a sacrament. By our baptism we are called to a priesthood of all believers. Further differentiation within the church was significant (in contrast to arbitrary or irrelevant), but was primarily functional. In this sense, our use of a functional approach to offices is an extension of our heritage.

19

But what is unique about the American experience is that we have applied a functional approach to everything — even to the church itself. Everything has meaning and value only as an instrument or means. Ordained ministry as well as structural parts of churches are understood functionally. For example, in the United Church of Christ, congregations are united first in associations and then in turn in a conference. Both the association and the conference are defined as territorial bodies to carry out functions. Since conferences and associations bear no substantive value with respect to the being of the church, their value is dependent on their ability to carry out functions.

The second theme drawn from Protestantism is the sovereignty of God. The application of this principle has always meant that nothing in this world is absolute, but that everything stands under judgment and that we all exist for the sake of God. Even in its affirmation of grace, which is the driving force of Protestantism, there is a built-in caution about objectifying grace in such a way that human beings might claim too much for themselves or their practices. The God who is holy and gracious is always sovereign, and we need to be on guard against excessive claims. H. Richard Niebuhr referred to this as the Protestant dilemma.[7] Since life in this world requires that we create things and institutions, it is necessary to justify them as worthy of our work, imagination, and care. To preach a sermon, to teach a class, to ask someone to join this church, to build a church or conduct the annual stewardship drive — all of these acts presume that what is done is worthy of attention. But can we do these things without challenging the sovereignty of God? Will we claim too much and thereby imply that the act is so sacred that it is above criticism, or even allows dictatorial or oppressive strategies?

Religious functionalism fits into the classic Protestant mind-

7. H. Richard Niebuhr, *The Kingdom of God in America* (New York: Harper and Row, 1937), 28-44.

set so easily because it borrows the principle of the sovereignty of God. The distinction between the world and God is applied to the distinction of means and ends. The church dares not speak of itself as an end, because only God is the true end. Therefore the church is a means. Worship, preaching, fellowship, offices, education, and structures are means to a greater end: the coming of the Rule of God. The activist church, using both the Enlightenment and Protestant sources, is the perfect expression of this religious functionalism. It affirms functionalism to acquire leverage against an uncritical status quo (i.e., that the church is not an end but a means), but also to keep its eye on the true ultimate end, which is the Rule of God.

The argument, then, is that religious functionalism in America has two sources: the cultural tradition stemming from the Enlightenment, which was so influential in the formation of our nation in the eighteenth century, and the application of key Protestant themes, which provided religious justification. If there is any doubt that these two traditions have come together to create a distinctive mind-set, one can compare mainline, liberal Protestant traditions with conservative Protestantism or liberal Catholicism. Conservative Protestants have been sheltered from the full force of both the Enlightenment and Protestantism. They are not as suspicious of institutions, and their individualism has always been checked by traditional loyalty to creeds or Bible. Liberal Catholics have been spared the excesses of individualism and possess a spirituality that affirms the being of the church and sacraments. Their activism is still in the context of orthodox faith and worship. But in liberal Protestantism, the two traditions have merged, producing a form of religion that is both individualistic and functional.

Our conclusion is that if individualism is the form of American religion, functionalism is its substance. It exists to do something. Herein we find the triumph of doing over being. There is, however, great irony in this triumph. The chief exponents of functionalism are leaders and writers representing an activist view of the church, which defines the church in terms of acts of love and justice. A new generation, schooled in liberation theology, speaks of praxis. These voices join together in the critique of the Enlightenment and boldly speak of the end of the Modern Age. Yet it was the last and greatest advocate of the Enlightenment who could accept no definition of religion other than one that reduced it to a form of moral action. Kant declared that since we cannot know God in terms of demonstrable, worldly knowledge, God could still be affirmed as a corollary to the moral life. This Kantian solution to the problem of religion for the modern mind has persisted through the liberal religious tradition. Religion can and must be justified by its moral usefulness. The triumph of doing over being is in fact the heritage of the Enlightenment.

For the liberal church, the gain in this shift to doing is that it gives the church a way to speak to the world in a language the world understands. A liberal church accepts the social/political language of the culture. The loss of such a shift is that authority for the church is defined strictly in terms of moral witness, rather than theological or spiritual witness. The church is thus in danger of being one dimensional, cut off from its history, its theology, and its own language.

Several contemporary expressions of religious functionalism will illustrate the extent of this transformation of Christian faith. The first has to do with the way denominations define themselves. Craig Dykstra and James Hudnut-Beumler argue that American denominational systems represent various models of organization.[8] Since the late nineteenth century the dom-

8. Craig Dykstra and James Hudnut-Beumler, "The National Organizational Structures of Protestant Denominations: An Invitation to a Conversation," in *The Organizational Revolution: Presbyterians and American Denominationalism,* ed. Milton J Coalter, John M. Mulder, and Louis B. Weeks (Louisville: Westminster/John Knox Press, 1992), 307-31.

inant form has been that of a corporate entity, dispensing goods and services. They also suggest that this form is being replaced by that of a regulatory agency (e.g., establishing standards for ministry). This theory confirms Bellah's thesis that institutions in America are functional: national structures exist for no reason other than to provide goods and services. In a sense, regulation is also a service, though it also has an episcopal concern for the being of the church. To refer again to the regional bodies in the United Church of Christ, conferences are defined in functional terms to do things for pastors and churches. The same can be said for the UCC national agencies, which are even named *instrumentalities!* But when you arrive at the period of social conflict and alienation between national agencies and local churches, a crisis occurs. Congregations find themselves rejecting the goods and services of regional and national bodies. Decisions about curriculum, hymnals, general resources, consultants, and even new pastors are made by the congregations according to interest and need. While this reaction may violate traditional denominational expectations, it is quite appropriate for the corporate model. In free-market functionalism, if people do not want the goods and services, it is appropriate to reject them and even shop around. More important, there is nothing left to tie individuals and congregations to the national structures. At the other end, the officers who defined themselves as providers of goods and services have lost their reason for being.

A second expression has to do with the dominant cultural view of religion. It may be called Add-On Religion. For middle- and upper-class America, the individual exists as a social, economic entity, creating the form and content of life for oneself and/or family. Since religion is understood as doing something, religion is used to add on certain things to one's life: contact with people, personal assistance in moral or spiritual growth, assistance in child rearing or family problems, social status, or even participation in programs that transcend the ordinary. The self is the center of this religion, choosing what will contribute to personal happiness, well-being, and meaning. Since churches have discovered that this is how people think, they are tempted to respond in kind. I once heard a sermon on Paul's affirmation of the variety of gifts and the unity of the church that included a lengthy analysis of each gift. It then concluded with the admonition: "So go home and consider how these gifts can make you a better person." Up until then I had no idea that Paul was thinking about personal enrichment. But in a functional worldview, even a discussion of the unity of the church can be a way to add something to individuals searching for individual happiness and meaning.

Finally we need to acknowledge the blatant Pelagianism of functionalism. If religion is about doing, then the person is the chief actor and everything will depend on what this person does. Do you believe? Have you done the right things? So much of American revivalism, which through television has become part of popular religion in America, places all of the burden of one's salvation on the individual's belief. If you believe, salvation and all manner of good things will happen to you. When this view takes control of believer's baptism, then baptism is no longer a response to grace but a work of the believer. In its most sinister form, it suggests to the sick that they have not been healed because of their unbelief, for if they had only believed, God would have healed them. Functionalism is ultimately overbearing in its demands and lacking in grace. It replaces trust in a gracious God with reliance on our own actions.

Beyond Individualism and Functionalism

The church seldom analyzes its problems in religious terms. Instead it seeks psychological and organizational motifs for

24

analysis and renewal. It also focuses on individual acts rather than structural issues or historic patterns of institutional life. Too often churches would rather blame the pastor than admit they have been affected by broader forces. The problems of individualism and functionalism are spiritual and theological in nature, which have become part of historical patterns of institutional life. Moreover, the problems are not simply wrong versus right, but the glorious ambivalence caused by excess, the half-truth, and the preoccupation with the current need. What is required is a theological reform, directed more at ourselves than against ritual enemies. We need less a rejection of certain concerns and passions than a reform of them, enabling us to see both sides and the whole truth.

Ecumenical or mainstream Protestantism is caught in a strange dilemma: on the one hand it affirms a religious history and theology that is thoroughly communal. It speaks of a social gospel, which pits it against individualistic piety. On the other hand, it appears incapable of breaking with basic tenets of American culture. Its preoccupation with the freedom of the individual and fear of institutions prevents it from affirming the faith and order essential for community. To some extent this can be explained historically, since liberal traditions stand guard against external repression and celebrate great moments of liberation from tyrannical forces. If German Protestants carry around the image of Luther nailing the Ninety-five Theses to the church door, English nonconformists remember the *Mayflower.* But can history explain it all? Is it not more of a spiritual matter, indeed, perhaps the quintessential American heresy: to posit oneself as free and innocent, self-made and needing no one, endlessly pursuing one's own happiness.

We will not resolve the dilemma without recognizing that certain elements of the culture and Protestantism have been so distorted that they themselves have become barriers to freedom as well as life together. It is not freedom but bondage to posit the self or the local congregation as basic and autonomous. One cannot add a communal perspective on to this type of individualism. One must start again; in fact, one must start from the place one wishes to go. Only if we start with the unity of the self with other selves in community can we move beyond the isolation of individualism. In fact this is precisely what the religious tradition does. Virtually every major part of the Bible presents us with persons in community — whether it be celebration or struggle. All of the images of sin and salvation are social. Moreover, the same can be said of post-Enlightenment social theory. Since the eighteenth century most social theory does in fact begin with the social unit as primary, speaking of the individual in relation to community. It is commonplace to recognize that the individual self becomes a person only in relation to other persons. Contemporary social theory is so committed to the social character of our life that in many cases it is deterministic! Does anyone today propose a social theory that begins by positing the free, rational, individual self? Yet the liberal tradition in America persists in its individualism and anti-institutionalism.

A movement away from such individualism brings unforeseen benefits. One is the reclaiming of the word *personal*. American religion has always emphasized religion as personal experience. Liberals have been quite ready to speak in these terms when attacking notions of religion as abstract ideas or second-hand doctrines. But they have always been nervous when popular evangelists say, "You must have a personal relation with Jesus." In such contexts, *personal* suggests private piety and subjectivism. But what if the personal is always persons in relation, involving responsibility and accountability? If we could speak of the personal in relational terms, we would avoid much of the individualism. Relational language goes well with egalitarian standards; it is easy to understand in horizontal terms rather than the vertical images of hierarchy. What if baptism placed us in relation to other baptized persons, all sharing a calling? In an age where the personal has been so abused, it may very well be that images of the church as personal may help to recover the reality of our corporate life.

The tradition also offers resources that allow us to see beyond functionalism. Here it is important to draw on the religious tradition, because functionalism has been so well defended by religious principles. The first and most immediate help comes from a prophetic protest against the way functionalism dehumanizes life. If all that we do is instrumental — a means to an end — then it has value only to the extent that it enables us to achieve that end. Such functionalism separates doing from being and threatens to devalue every act and person. Do we really want to say to those gathered in worship, "Let us now pray, but please remember that this prayer is only a means to some end." Is every act of friendship, service, or study only a means? Are preaching, evangelism, stewardship, and witness all to be judged as means? Is there no sense in which these acts embody the presence of God and are of value in and of themselves?[9]

A second source of reform is the eschatological character of Jesus' teachings. We do not have to choose between means and ends, present and future, being and doing. An eschatological reading makes clear that Jesus declares that the rule of God is now and looks to the coming of God's glory. It is here now in the flowers of the field and the divine care of all things; it

9. Current seminarians present an interesting paradox. In general, many of them are more spiritually mature than my generation of thirty years ago. They are older, have experienced the trials of life, and come to seminary with a clear sense of the presence of God in their lives, calling them to ministry. But when asked to define the mission of the church, they readily speak in terms of means and ends: the church's purpose is to witness to the coming of the Rule of God. It is as if their ecclesiology has not caught up with their spirituality. Or perhaps it is the contrast between an activist theology and their own personal sense of the presence of God.

is also coming to make all things new. In this sense, things can have both *present* and *future* value, *embody* grace and *point* to a future grace, *possess substantive* and *functional value*. Things, actions, and people embody now the presence of God and are to be used for God's glory. From this perspective, our obsession with doing and means is half right, but we have treated it as the whole truth. It is also half wrong in its refusal to talk about the church in language of substance and being.

A third help is found when we acknowledge that functionalism is affirmed more for critical, rather than positive, reasons. Protestants tend to see the alternative to functionalism as a move to invest things in the present with substantive value and power. That immediately raises the issue of sanctifying acts and policies, offices and institutions. It also connects with our memory of exclusive hierarchies and tyranny. Functionalism has been the ready defense against things we oppose (even though we may have forgotten what they are).

How can an egalitarian and inclusive church embrace a substantive view of things, if that view is so identified with hierarchy and exclusive practices? Will such a church not lose its critical leverage against oppression and grow soft on its affirmation of equality? If the question must be framed in these terms, then there may be no other option than the current choice that pits a functional, egalitarian church against a substantive, hierarchical one. But what if the issue can be completely reframed? What if we can join together egalitarian values with substantive values? What if we reject the idea that a substantive view always leads to hierarchy and egalitarianism can be maintained only by functionalism?

From the view of the heritage, the answer is obvious: the New Testament is full of examples where substantive and egalitarian values are joined together. The primary one is the Lord's Supper (and the new covenant it represents). It is at once a substantive relation, involving the real presence of Jesus Christ for our salvation, and also a radically egalitarian act: in Christ there is neither Jew nor Gentile, rich nor poor, slave nor free, male nor female. This egalitarianism is also present in baptism, which has never been withheld from any person because of race, gender, class, ethnicity, or physical or mental incapacity. In both sacraments, egalitarianism is united with a substantive affirmation. Yet another example is the way Christian worship is liberated from all hierarchy and restrictions as to time and place: "Wherever two or three gather in my name, there am I. . . ." The Lord's Supper can be celebrated anyplace and anytime, thereby affirming the universal and free presence of Christ.

Finally, consider the issue of *office*. The church has established offices on the assumption that there are certain things essential to its very nature. These offices have both a substantive and a functional character: they embody something essential in the church's life (e.g., teaching, preaching, administration of the sacraments, pastoral care), and they represent a duty or function to be accomplished. The word *office* illustrates the point: *officium* refers to the performance of duty. That sounds very functional, until you think about the duty. The office is designed not to do *anything*, but a *particular* thing. Since the duty represents something of value, the word can refer to the value itself, such as a service, ceremony, or rite. The office has authority because it is connected to something of value as well as the responsibility to fulfill the duty. What we find here is a certain dialectic at work: neither substantive nor functional views alone can completely define an office. Can someone claim to be a preacher who never preaches? Being must find expression in doing. But just as untenable is preaching that says nothing, or something contrary to the gospel. Action unrelated to substance is inherently self-destructive.

The question Protestants need to ask is whether the functional definition of office, and even the church itself, has been so completely separated from the substantive view that it is a new distortion. The sixteenth-century reform was aimed against the hierarchy of religious orders, seeking to open the church to all the baptized. In this sense ordination was a rite rather than a sacrament, suggesting functions essential to the life of the church. But even within this view, the offices set aside for ordination retain a substantive character, derived from the task itself. For example, the teaching office can only be understood substantively and functionally. There is a datum of the teaching office that is objectively given: "For I delivered to you as of first importance what I also received." It is impossible to speak of the teaching office without implying a normative teaching. At the same time, the teaching office implies a function. Teachers are to teach, and we can even expect them to do so effectively. In a Protestant spirit, one can say, "Anyone who does what teachers are supposed to do is a teacher." But in a Catholic spirit, one can add, "One can teach only if one is a part of the new being of Jesus Christ." A teacher is defined by both the action of teaching and the reality of the gospel, which is embodied in persons and must be shared.

To conclude: our argument is that the problems facing American churches are more than the periodic lapses of faith or vision, or the inevitable ineffectiveness of organizational programs that have run their course. American religion has developed in quite specific ways. Our culture has formed religion in structural ways that affect the way we think of religion and the church, as well as ways we organize and operate our institutions. At the most fundamental level, individualism and functionalism represent spiritual or theological affirmations about the individual and his/her relation to Christ and the church. These affirmations are distortions of human values and community. In this chapter we have made suggestions in a preliminary way as to how theological reform might redefine faith and the church. In Chapters Four and Five we will take up this theological reconstruction.

CHAPTER 2

Images of the Church

Pluralism is the dominant characteristic of American Christianity, and it has always been this way. There has always been a diversity of ethnicity, race, class, region, and religious persuasion. What is new about the current experience of pluralism is that it is as much internal to each church family (denomination) as a reality dividing churches. One expects to encounter foreign traditions and practices when meeting persons from other denominations. The new experience of pluralism takes place at one's own annual conference or synod. Moreover, the differences are often so great that they constitute a difference in kind. Opposite views on evangelism, worship, social issues, education, church order, and ministry point to a more radical separation. General discussion is difficult, if not impossible, precisely because participants speak different theological languages and appeal to alternative authorities.

This experience of pluralism exposes a plurality of ecclesiologies. It is in our views of the church that broad affirmations of God, Christ, sin, and salvation take form in the life and practice of communities. Yet we seldom discuss ecclesiology in the face of urgent debates over social issues, budgets, and

31

church politics. In spite of this neglect, all of the tensions and disputes over theology and praxis reflect fundamental assumptions about the church's nature and purpose. How we think about the church both reflects and determines how we think and act on most other things.

Constructing a Typology of the Church

To understand the divergence among churches in contemporary Christianity, I have constructed a typology focusing on the concept *apostolic*. Every Christian claims to be apostolic, that is, commissioned or sent by Christ. But what defines one as apostolic? Each type represents an answer to this question of what is absolutely essential for the church to be the church. Each one rests on a primary image that authorizes a form of the church and provides a vision of its life and mission. Thus each tradition lives with confidence, even in the face of other traditions that answer the question of apostolicity in different terms.

This is not the first time a typology regarding the church has been developed. In 1953 Lesslie Newbigin set forth a threefold analysis of Western Christianity, represented by the Catholic, Lutheran/Calvinist, and Anabaptist traditions.[1] This analysis was helpful in understanding how these three traditions could all claim to be genuinely Christian and yet be so divided. Newbigin's analysis also opened the way for asking how the three traditions complement each other, rather than simply exclude each other.

In 1978 Avery Dulles proposed a fivefold analysis of church types: (1) institution; (2) mystical communion; (3) sac-

1. Cf. Lesslie Newbigin, *The Household of God* (New York: Friendship Press, 1953).

rament; (4) herald (i.e., proclamation); (5) servant.[2] Dulles assumes that the church is a mystery, based on the "divine self-gift."[3] From this perspective, he then argues that one cannot speak of the church in analytic, categorical language. Instead one must speak by way of analogies, models, and images that reflect and point to the reality of the church. "When an image is employed reflectively and critically to deepen one's theoretical understanding of a reality it becomes what is today called a 'model.'"[4] He concludes that a model becomes a paradigm when it is used to formulate a comprehensive ecclesiology. Models or paradigms thus become images of the church. Their positive and negative values can be analyzed. They can be compared and hopefully reconciled, since Dulles assumes that each contributes something positive and cannot be dismissed. In the expanded edition of 1987, he includes a chapter on "The Church: Community of Disciples," where he presents his own constructive attempt to reconcile the five models.[5]

The typology presented here differs from Dulles's in several decisive ways. First, the five models Dulles presents are in the main conceptual constructs developed by theologians. The obvious exception is the first, which Dulles uses to represent three centuries of the Roman Catholic Church up to Vatican II. But even here the references are to the writings of popes and other theologians, rather than to the way such a model finds expression in the faith, life, and practice of a church. In the description of the church as mystical communion (the second model), there are no references to religious orders, which embody this model in a marvelous way. Instead

2. Avery Dulles, *Models of the Church,* expanded ed. (New York: Doubleday, 1987).
3. Dulles, 17.
4. Dulles, 23.
5. Dulles, 204-26.

the references are to writers. The sacramental model is not illustrated by communities that have made this the heart of their faith and life, but is offered primarily as a way to resolve the tensions between the models of the church as institution and as mystical communion. In the model that would be more akin to Protestants (i.e., herald), the references are to Barth and Bultmann, rather than the Lutheran, Calvinist, or Free Churches that have created communities of faith sustained by proclamation for over four hundred years. The same holds for the servant model. There are no references to servant communities, but only to writers protesting the lack of concern for peace and justice.

A second problem is that in spite of Dulles's stated intention, all five models do not have the same value or status. In theory, each is to represent a positive element that needs to be incorporated into a truly comprehensive ecclesiology. But in fact the five are a mixed lot. The first (institution) is affirmed as representing the obvious need for institutional order and life in the world. But it is quickly identified with institutionalism and roundly rejected. As the dominant mark of the triumphalist church of Vatican I, it represents a model more to be opposed than affirmed. Later in his attempt to reconcile the five models, Dulles observes that of the five models, this one cannot be made primary in reconstructing ecclesiology.[6] Thus, while this model may point to a need for structure, it is largely a negative model.

In his treatment of the last two models, a mixed evaluation undercuts the confidence one might have in thinking of these models as organizing principles for real communities. The herald church is presented with strong biblical justification and ample references to twentieth-century theologians. Why Luther, Calvin, and Wesley are omitted is strange, but this again reflects Dulles's

6. Dulles, 198.

interest in the models as conceptual constructs for dialogue with other writers. But as soon as the validity of this kerygmatic form is affirmed, the traditional Roman Catholic criticism is introduced to remind us that a church cannot live by words alone. Whether this criticism is appropriate to the writers Dulles uses (Barth and Bultmann) is a debate that will never end. But how does it relate to those real communities that have endured for centuries, insisting that their faith and practice be governed by the gospel proclamation? Can a model judged to be so flawed actually function in a typology of churches?

A similar ambivalence occurs in the presentation of the servant model, only it is more complicated. First, the servant model is complicated by the combination of two elements: self-sacrificial service and an openness to the modern world (viewed as a form of service). The latter element reflects Dulles's repudiation of the triumphalism of Vatican I, and symbolizes a dialogical relation to the modern world, with its new knowledge and freedoms. But these two elements are not always joined together in the real world. By linking these two elements in one model, Dulles makes the entire model vulnerable to the traditional criticism of any embrace of the modern world that loses its moorings in the heritage. Thus the image of the diaconal church committed to service must bear the burden of the modernist controversy. Both Mother Teresa and the Mennonites would certainly ask why their vision of the church as a servant community is linked to the burden of modernism.

Second, the servant model is undercut by a criticism that needs far more elaboration than given by Dulles. After commending the servant model, Dulles notes that one objection to it is "its lack of any direct Biblical foundation."[7] He recognizes the primacy of service, love, and self-sacrifice in the New

7. Dulles, 99.

Testament, but argues that the New Testament does not connect these practices to the church's relation to the world. Given the broad themes of Jesus in the Sermon on the Mount, Mark 8 and 10, and the witness of the epistles in 1 Corinthians 13 or Philippians 2, this is a very narrow reading of the New Testament. Since Dulles sets the Bible as a standard for judging each model, the consequence is that here we have a model that fails, in Dulles's eyes, the first test of validity.

A third general problem with Dulles's typology is that it is constructed primarily from a Roman Catholic perspective. An opening is offered to Protestants in the herald and servant models, but, as we have seen, these models are dismissed rather quickly. Indeed, how could Protestants take a model seriously if it were not biblical, as Dulles argues in the case of the servant model. But equally important, many Protestants would be hard pressed to identify with any of these models. The Anabaptist and Pentecostal traditions, the African-American churches, and even those traditions focusing on the Gathered Church image would find it difficult to locate themselves in these five options.

This review of Dulles's approach gives opportunity to highlight the distinctive features of the typology offered here. First, these images of the church represent real communities. They are embodied in the major traditions in the American experience. We can abstract from these traditions to create a conceptual framework for constructing an ideal ecclesiology. But in the first instance our goal is to understand the different organizing principles that inspire such radical diversity.

Second, all eight images in this typology are positive images of the church. None is a caricature of a flawed ecclesiology, presented for the sake of rejection. In this respect we agree with Dulles's intention: each represents a positive aspect that must ultimately be incorporated into a truly ecumenical view of the church. The initial presentation of each image in its positive form does not, however, overlook that each can be and has been corrupted. If evil is the corruption of the good, rather than its absence, each model embodied in historic traditions will reveal a distinctive corruption. These will be noted, and, in our reflections on the use of the typology, will be an important factor in understanding the dynamics between the traditions.

Third, this typology will seek to incorporate the dominant traditions in American Christianity. To this end the original three models from Newbigin needed to be expanded and subdivided. In presentations of this typology in its early versions, it became evident that expansion was needed to include all of the listeners. Thus the original three have become eight and will probably continue to grow. We turn then to eight images, as distinctive definitions of the essence of the church.

Eight Images of the Church

An examination of the way Christians think about the church reveals multiple forms or images that express what is essential. This typology presents eight definitions of apostolicity. Each view is descriptive as well as prescriptive, that is, an appeal to authority. In our presentation of each image we shall enumerate basic assumptions, locate the principle of authority, and describe the view of mission. We shall also note how this form can become negative or flawed.

1. Sacramental Participation in the Historic Community

The title for this view combines two elements. Some would argue that they should be separate, as does Dulles when he divides the sacramental from the institutional model. But as an image of the essence of the church, they are really one. Eastern Orthodox, Roman Catholics, and Episcopalians and other high-church Protestants experience the mystery of Christianity through the unity of the two. Worship and faith involve a spiritual or sacramental life, wherein believers are united with Christ and one another. This spiritual reality is, without question, the reality confessed and handed down through the ages by the church of the apostles. The sacraments would be questioned if not administered by those authorized by Christ. Sacramental grace always finds expression in real communities that witness to, nurture, and celebrate the Christian life. By contrast, those in authority have no power except that derived from their relation to the saving grace of Jesus Christ. The institutional authority must always be tied to the grace of the sacraments.

At the heart of this view is the celebration of the incarnation, which continues in the world through the presence of the resurrected Christ and the Holy Spirit. The Christian life, therefore, is not an idea, but participation in a new spiritual reality that is in tension with the fallen powers of this world. Life is structured and ordered by grace. Discipleship is a process of spiritual formation in the image of Christ. All of this is experienced in relation to the historic community that exists with its traditions, bishops, and practices. Indeed, one cannot be a Christian except through participation (i.e., being connected) in this church. Thus American Catholics have a natural and delightful idiom: they define themselves as to whether they are *practicing* Catholics. A Protestant would never think of saying that! And of course, that says a great deal about both Catholics and Protestants.

It follows that authority resides in the representatives of Christ (bishops), who are given oversight of the church. This authority is lodged in the offices, structures, and laws of the church. But it is ultimately tied to the saving power of the gospel and sacraments. In practice such authority can be divided and tilt one way or another: toward the institution or the gospel. The history of struggle between the bishops and the theologians illustrates the point.

The church's mission is to be the Body of Christ and to extend it throughout the world. The celebration of the sacraments is the focal point of worship, since they represent the mystery of God's saving presence. The primacy given to the sacraments and spirituality has emphasized the ordained clergy, and in some traditions religious orders. This has tended to emphasize the distinction of the church and the world, as well as a hierarchy within the church. All of these elements (sacraments, orders, and hierarchy) make it clear that the church's mission is to be a community on earth: to actualize the new being of Jesus Christ, to be the means of grace to a world in need.

History has revealed, however, that churches living within this orientation are subject to temptations. It is possible for a sacramental system to become mechanical, for the emphasis on practice (doing) to become legalistic and moralistic. Moreover, those entrusted with such sacred authority too easily equate the church in its organizational and cultural traditions with divine authority itself. It is no secret that authoritarianism and institutionalism have been the negative forms of this image, no matter what denominational context is involved.

2. *Confessing the True Faith*

This image of the church has a twofold origin: it is as much a protest against current practice and traditions as it is a desire to be renewed by the Word of God in Jesus Christ. Participation in the sacramental system and acceptance of the current authority of the church are subordinated to the authority of the gospel, which is affirmed as the sole foundation for the church. Here appeals are made to the long tradition of criticism in the prophets and Jesus. It is illustrated by Luther in his first thesis, which defined the Christian life as one of continual repentance. Every form of human pride, be it religious arrogance, the abuse of power, or the attempts to control God through human thought or action, must be shattered. But repentance is only a clearing of our minds and hearts that we might stand once again before the God who is gracious and wills life. It is this sovereignty of God — as judgment against human pretension and grace unconditionally given — that constitutes the central theme of this image. The church can only be the church when it acknowledges that its entire existence is grounded in the gracious action of God. Hearing, understanding, and acting on this Word constitute the essence of the Christian life.

For this image the central issue of religion is trust of the heart. We love, trust, and hope either in God or in something else. Moreover, it is this true trust that determines our proper thought and action. The obsession of this tradition with true faith is not a bias toward theory or doctrine, but a consequence of Jesus' teaching that only a good tree bears good fruit. Only if the church claims the gospel as its sole treasure will it be faithful and know the promises of God. It follows that authority will be lodged in Scripture, as the record and witness to God's saving act, as well as the divinely inspired Word that transcends, judges, and reorders all human words. Church order, traditions, and offices are all under the authority of Scripture. But as Luther soon discovered, it was too broad simply to claim Scripture. Scripture must be interpreted by some guide. For Luther this standard was the sovereignty of God's grace, as well as the creeds.

On these terms the church's mission is to be faithful in its witness against all of the principalities and powers of this world. It is to stand firm in the proclamation of grace in the face of every false claim to security. The church is a community ordered by grace, where faith is active in love. The breaking with the hierarchy and conventions of religious life in the sixteenth century was only the critical side of this mission. Its real power was in the new sense of the calling of every Christian, by virtue of baptism, to claim his or her Christian vocation in the world in service of God and neighbor.

This form of the church takes on a negative cast when it allows the center to move from personal trust in God to the principles derived from the essential impulse. Instead of the centrality of grace, this form has allowed the Bible and/or doctrine to become absolute, finding security in the literalism of these texts. The focus on justification has also produced a serious division between justification and sanctification. Strange things happen when the faith and practice of communities are guided solely by a word of acceptance and less by the call to become the community of love and justice. Bonhoeffer's charge of cheap grace can be lodged only against a tradition that has allowed grace to make it content with a sinful status quo. While this criticism is usually directed toward the Lutheran tradition, it also applies to Calvinism. Even here, with its more vigorous tradition of social reform, there is caution at taking seriously the demands and promise of sanctification. In contemporary America the religion of grace, so desperately needed, is inevitably reduced to a blessing of the status quo and the quest for personal happiness.

3. Rebirth in the Spirit

Since images in this typology are drawn from actual communities, it is not surprising that they should live in protest against one another. Whereas the first claims the authority of the historic community as the means of grace, the second seeks to reorder the church by the gospel itself. But both still rely on broad, formal structures. Both are accepting of state churches, emphasize ordained ministries as authoritative teachers and preachers, practice infant baptism, and rely heavily on the creeds. Against such an array of formalism and political power, the third image of the church is born of the Spirit in individuals and small communities. It affirms that the church can consist only of persons born again and empowered with new life. Faith is a choice one must make: to be baptized and receive the Spirit. It is a call to forsake the world and be transformed by the power of the Holy Spirit.

Communities formed by spiritual rebirth have developed in a variety of ways, especially in America. For the most part, all share believers' baptism and a rejection of formalized religion and reliance on creeds, affirming the teachings of Jesus and the expectation of new possibilities in the Spirit. In the Anabaptist traditions this image of the church has focused on intense practice of the Christian life in prayer, study of the Bible, communal associations, service, and a rejection of violence and worldliness. In Baptists and Pentecostals it has evolved into traditions that emphasize faith as personal decision, the Bible as the primary rule for faith and practice, and vigorous programs of evangelism.

In all of these groups, authority stems from Scripture, with a focus on the teachings of Jesus and the presence of the Holy Spirit. Since genuine religion involves rebirth in the Spirit, in contrast to formal and established religion, authority must be based on demonstration of new life. If Lutheranism and Calvinism are characterized as religions of grace, these traditions may be described as the religion of power. One can expect something now of God; believers can and must grow in new life.

It follows that mission will be understood in terms of the witness to new life and demonstrations of it in the world. There will be a broad spectrum of views as to how this mission is practiced and where it should be focused. For the Anabaptists, it takes the form of radical opposition to war and extensive programs of world service. For others with a more individualistic interpretation, mission is directed toward evangelism and personal holiness.

The problems arising in this broad tradition may be divided into two areas. Since it has a strong separatist or sectarian tendency, especially in the Anabaptist peace churches, it has been in a continuous debate with the majority of Protestants. At stake is not simply the question of participation in military action, but general participation in the world and the possibility of transforming the very structures and powers of the world. While Anabaptists do not see their position as a flaw, but their very purpose for being, the other Protestants and Catholics have been unable to accept it as a formative principle for the church. The other area where problems arise is in the individualism of this form, especially as worked out in the history of Pentecostalists, Baptists, and other Free Churches. This manifests itself in its tendency to disassociate itself from the history of the church and rely on individual claims to authority conferred by the Spirit. The history of revivalism arising from these groups has often been characterized by excessive emotionalism and the manipulation of people. The irony of all this has been that a tradition arising out of the impulse to separate from culture ends up embracing culture, as represented by the charismatic leader or local traditions.

4. Acts of Love and Justice or Right Action

In this view of *apostolic,* acts of love and justice constitute the rule of life for the church and the ultimate test of the Christian life. This is based on the teachings of Jesus and other testimonies to the primacy of love (e.g., the Gospel and Letters of John). Along with this substantive norm, this view carries the assumption that true religion manifests itself in right action. These two factors together constitute a critical principle, denouncing any religion defined as ideas or doctrines. There is here an opposition to all hypocrisy, legalism, and self-serving institutionalism. Both the prophets and Jesus offer examples of both types of criticism.

Authority in this form of the church is the scriptural mandate for justice, mercy, and love. Persons claiming authority for leadership must demonstrate it by their capacity for prophetic insight into the contemporary world and their ability to envision a new world of love and justice. It follows that the mission of the church will be to discern the true meaning of love and justice, as well as their application to the church and the world. This prompts persons in this tradition to move constantly to new applications, frontiers, and areas where oppression hampers or destroys freedom and life. The key will be the ability to engage in acts of love and justice, and thereby embody the self-sacrificial life of Jesus. Perhaps the text used most often for this image is Matthew 25, with its double affirmation: discipleship means acts of love, mercy, and justice; in doing these acts to those in need we encounter Jesus himself.

This image of the church becomes flawed when its moral passion is so intense that it moves toward moralism and legalism. While contemporary usage has coined the phrase "political correctness," social and legal control have been part of moral reform movements for a long time. Moral reform movements of the left or right have always been tempted by intolerance and oppressive measures. The other major problem with this form lies not in what it affirms but in what is left out. A Christian community cannot be sustained over time simply on the theme of right action. There are other theological themes that are central to the faith, without which right action becomes obsessive and self-destructive, lacking grace and forgiveness. The fact is that the church's life holds other moments besides service: worship, teaching, care, fellowship, aesthetic/artistic expression, spiritual life, evangelism, stewardship — to name the most basic. The single-mindedness of this image too often produces a meteoric life span, burning out for lack of substance.

5. *Confessing Our Unity in Christ (World Unity)*

This image defines the church as both a witness to and an embodiment of the unity God creates in Jesus Christ. The appeal here is to the incarnation as the beginning of a new age: God is uniting all things in Christ. Against all human divisions, but especially the divisions of the church, this image has little patience for our acceptance of such divisions and the human suffering caused by them. In our time this image has been given new energy in the emerging global perspective, which makes national and denominational perspectives obsolete. What arises is a new internationalism of Christians, built on personal encounters throughout the world in service projects, conferences, and partnerships.

Authority will be defined in terms of biblical affirmations of unity, from creation to the great commission. The Johannine images of unity will receive special attention. These scriptural texts are confirmed by an appeal to the experience of unity throughout the world in faith, worship, service, and fellowship. Persons in this tradition have usually been transformed by experiences of suffering and celebration in world Christianity. The church's mission will be to participate in this process of unifying all things in Christ. The modern worldwide ecumenical movement continues to inspire this image of the church. It has also opened up a completely new type of ecumenicity involving Christianity and other religions. This new encounter has raised as many questions as answers, since it requires a much different perspective and language than that traditionally involved in intra-Christian dialogues.

The problems with this image may be more in the eye of the beholder than in the object itself. Global Christians often appear preoccupied with the vision of world unity and detached from the concrete issues and problems of particular churches. In a culture where Christianity is still defined and practiced primarily in denominational patterns, many are not sure how they can maintain the integrity of such patterns and at the same time move out into a new world of global Christianity. This model is thus perceived as relinquishing particular standards and traditions, which often were part of the very origin of the tradition. When the move toward unity becomes identified with a mandate for action growing out of the model of Right Action, ecumenical progress becomes something to do in spite of concern for resolving theological and liturgical differences. Those involved in such ecumenical ventures soon find themselves isolated from their original constituencies. If ecumenical leaders can get too far ahead of their people in these matters, it is all the more so when the discussion shifts to encounters with world religions. Here a new realm presents even more questions and concerns. At issue is the need to affirm the distinctiveness and authority of Christian faith in the face of the reality of living in an interdependent global situation. In its commitment to throw off the old colonial imperialism of Western churches, too often this tradition has not been able to give a clear and definite answer to the concerns raised, which ultimately constitute the Christological question. But it must be said in fairness to these ecumenical pilgrims that the critics too often speak out of the protected isolation of home communities and display little regard for what has been actually happening in the world.

6. The Covenant Community or Gathered Church

Here the church is truly the church when it gathers as a community of faith, worship, fellowship, and service. The key is the need to actualize the church in a community that embodies the

46

Christian life. Unlike the third model (Rebirth in the Spirit), this tradition is not always ignited by the rejection of infant baptism or by Pentecostal fervor. It is more likely motivated by a rejection of state churches and external structures. There is also an implied notion that the covenant community stands against the world. English nonconformists (e.g., Congregationalists and Presbyterians) rejected the tyranny of bishops and the state. Most Pietist movements live with the tension between the church and the world. African-American churches, rejected by most white churches, created communities of faith against a hostile world, wherein faith, fellowship, and freedom might flourish.

In this tradition authority is lodged in Scripture, with an emphasis on the church as an independent community. The church's mission is to be faithful in its life together and witness in the world. Such churches see themselves actualizing the New Testament ideal. This ethos and vision of church life means leapfrogging over centuries of Christian history in order to restore the purity of early Christianity. To Catholics or Lutherans these communities seem flagrantly to disregard doctrinal history. But for them this criticism is not relevant. The key is to be the covenant community, gathered together and bound by the New Testament.

This description contains within it the elements that are easily abused. Individual congregations can become isolated and retreat into a self-serving form of existence. They can also be impoverished by pretending to connect with the first century without the experience of other ages of Christian development. In America this model has produced the idea of the autonomous local congregation, a notion derived from Lockean individualism and nineteenth-century liberalism. Doctrine, order, mission, and worship are determined by self-governing congregations. This tendency, which is increasing, gives expression to the dominant individualism of American religion. It is impossible to justify absolute independence of a person or congregation on theological grounds. Moreover, most Christians have acknowledged that the unity we share in Christ must and can be actualized in visible forms beyond the gathered community.[8]

7. Pilgrims and Seekers

This image calls believers to leave the security of formal, established systems of religion and journey as pilgrims and seekers. Like several other images, this one is born in protest against religion defined as institutional authority, doctrine, or legal codes. When these traditions become oppressive, seeking to stamp out individual freedom or impose abusive demands on people, there is usually an exodus. The victims of religious tyranny possess a refugee status. The memory of abuse tends to be formative for their religious consciousness. Often they carry this sense of flight for years after the withdrawal from oppressive systems. When they band together, it is in the

8. The concept of the autonomy of the local congregation can be approached both theologically and historically. In the former case, the word *autonomy* provokes strong reactions on both sides. Those critical of the concept point out that it has no warrant in the Bible or the tradition prior to its usage in English nonconformism. If God is sovereign, no person or congregation can be autonomous. Moreover, Christ did not reconcile us so that individuals or congregations can be autonomous. But for those supportive of the concept, it is a symbol of freedom from oppressive hierarchy and traditions. Such a defense shifts the focus to the historical perspective, where the Free Church tradition sees nothing but tyranny and bureaucratic logjams if the autonomy of the local church is lost. Perhaps one way out of this stalemate is to recognize that autonomy is more of a defensive position rather than the substantive, positive center of the Free Church. That is to say, it can be argued that the central affirmation of seventeenth- and eighteenth-century Congregationalism is the Lordship of Christ, not autonomy. The Lordship of Christ means freedom from kings and bishops, but not freedom to absolutize ourselves. Moreover, Christ the Lord also binds us together. There must be another way to guard against oppression and tyranny than by the concept of autonomy, which negates our unity in Christ.

conviction that true religion is the growth of the Spirit in the individual. There is usually an appeal to the transcendence and mystery of God, which leads to a rejection of lofty claims regarding doctrines and creeds, followed by a broad spirit of freedom, toleration, and inclusivity.

Authority will be defined in terms of writings and persons manifesting a genuine spiritual quest for truth. This includes Christian Scripture and documents, but is not limited to them, because God is always greater than one thing or tradition. The church's mission is to advance the spiritual quest, nurture freedom and truth among believers, and live in peace and justice with all people. The quest for truth — the journey — is as important as the goal. There is, therefore, a high toleration of individuality, dissent, and unresolved issues and a respect for limited answers.

While the pilgrim experience is normally a part of every Christian's life, it has proven unsatisfying for many when used as the sole standard. To be sure, Christianity affirms the sovereignty of the God who cannot be confined by human claims, concepts, and doctrines. But Christianity is ultimately defined by a cluster of affirmations that the majority have judged to be essential. This form of the church becomes problematic for most Christians when it refuses to accept closure on answers (some or all, depending on one's perspective), or when it introduces ideas from outside Christianity (positions judged heretical or ideas drawn from other religions). While this view of the church may be difficult for most Christians to imagine, the fact is that most congregations will probably have at least one person defined by this image.

8. Solidarity of Jesus with Those Who Suffer (Liberationist)

This image of the church is drawn from liberation theology. Some will ask why it is a separate model, since it could be seen as a twentieth-century version of Confessing the True Faith (see 2 above). Others in North America, raised in a tradition of liberal activism, will ask why it is not a part of the fourth model: Acts of Love and Justice. A strong case can be made for the former because it is a theological reform, rich in all of the major affirmations. Because it places praxis in the context of the entire faith and the worshiping community, it is usually much broader in scope than the activism of Right Action. But the main reason for a distinct place in this typology is that persons identifying with this image want it separate. Perhaps this illustrates the generation gap between the proponents of liberation theology and older liberal activists and/or neo-orthodox. It certain illustrates the power of language, as liberationists refuse to be allied with those of an earlier generation. Liberationists do not see themselves as a variation on other models, but a new image of the church.

Whether a completely new form or a close relative to others, this form appeals to the powerful themes of liberation theology: the protest against the church's identification with modern intellectual categories and the alignment of the church with oppressive political and economic structures, the hermeneutic of suspicion, the affirmation of the incarnation as the presence of God with the poor, and the priority of praxis. Authority is defined in terms of these new standards for understanding the gospel and its radical application to the liberation of oppressed peoples. The church's mission is to participate in the struggles for liberation among all who suffer. This includes the creation of communities of faith, where the solidarity with Jesus Christ and believers is actualized, as well as a witness wherever people are oppressed.

While no church has officially adopted a liberationist perspective, every ecumenical denomination has a strong representation of this perspective. These persons have utilized a liberationist theology to effect change and develop movements within and among denominations that give expression to this image of the church. Thus it is embodied in church life and practice, and is not simply an idea. But it may be too soon to evaluate this model since we have not seen it fully actualized over several generations in the full breadth of church life in North America.

The problems that have emerged thus far in North American Protestantism are similar to those in the fourth model (Acts of Love and Justice). A driving passion for justice can display signs of a higher righteousness and moralism. The hermeneutic of suspicion, as practiced in its popular form, ends up criticizing everyone but oneself. The conviction that God has identified with the poor too easily is translated into the claim that God has identified with my cause, analysis, and strategy. As a consequence this perspective can be as divisive as inclusive, as intimidating as liberating. At times one wonders if Latin and South American liberation theology has been co-opted by the traditional liberal theology that is so closely connected to American culture. This perspective has always been optimistic about individuals and suspicious of institutions, having a blind spot to individual self-deception but being overly cognizant of social evils. Nevertheless, liberation theology has resolved many of the old dichotomies in modern theology and has been a powerful force in the emerging global perspective of many churches.

The Typology at Work

To use this typology as a means for understanding how and why we differ, several things must be clarified.

First, the value of the classification is not in what it might uncover as to the origin and history of each group, but in the way it focuses attention on the relations between groups. By identifying different answers to the question of apostolicity, we

51

simultaneously see what is unique about each image as well as how and why it is different from all the others. When the classification is used in this way, it becomes quite apparent why Catholic, Lutheran, Pentecostal, liberal activist, and Gathered Church pastors approach issues in radically different ways. Indeed, one would expect them to differ! The starting points for thinking about Christ and the church are not easily reducible to a common or higher form of unity. It is in effect a difference in kind.

Second, the differences are complicated because we do not have eight forms of the church, but actually sixteen: eight positive forms and eight de-formations, or negative versions of the original images. In much debate, the argument pits a preferred positive form against one or more negative forms. In such a contest the forms represented by the negative versions are denounced, while the preferred positive is upheld as the victor. There will be no movement beyond such ritual warfare until we recognize the fallacy of such comparisons. Each of the eight — even my preferred — is corruptible. If the purpose of any discussion is to defend the flawed versions, no one shall stand.

Here it is appropriate to acknowledge that this cross-comparison of a positive versus a negative is deeply imbedded in our minds and hearts. This is because our thinking is in part determined by what we love (or value). And if we are determined by what we love, then we are also determined by what we fear and hate. Examine the list of negative forms. Which one represents a development that you despise or hate? Which one evokes from you deep-seated emotions of anger or fear?

Consider several examples. Recall how the relations between Catholics and Protestants up through the 1960s were determined as much by prejudice, fear, and hate as by reasoned theological arguments. Can a Lutheran or Calvinist really understand a Pentecostal, if such a person is interpreted by means of the excesses of TV religion? Can a liberationist understand the Gathered Church, if such a church is understood in terms of the racism and classism of our society? The point is that each image of the church bears a terrible burden, wherein what was created in love as a vision of the Christian life has become its very antithesis. We will not understand ourselves or be able to relate to other forms of the church unless we are honest about the way the negative forms shape our thinking and restrict any openness to mutual understanding.

Third, the eight types are drawn from Christian churches, representing broad traditions, movements, or denominations. But the types also represent individuals or local churches within denominations clearly identified with one type. It is not a surprise to suggest that all eight types are in most ecumenical denominations. In fact, the acrimonious debates within denominations have moved many to the brink of schism. We can extend the same logic and observe that all eight may be in each person. Like the Myers-Briggs categories, which are all present in each person but configured in different ways, with different characteristics dominant, so the eight images may also take shape within us in particular ways. Just as a denomination or congregation may have a profile, with one or more dominant images, some occasionally active, and one or more acting as ritual enemy, so such a profile may exist in each person.

With these clarifications, we can use the typology to analyze the polarizations that have become commonplace in American religious life. For example, in the United Church of Christ multiple definitions of the church are at work. The national boards and agencies are dominated by the fourth image: Acts of Love and Justice. The major exception is the World Board, which appears to represent the fifth model (World Unity), though it tends to merge this image with that of Right Action. Local congregations, depending on their history, identify with True Faith or the Covenant Community. Some high-church congregations identify with the Sacramental model, while some liberal activist congregations claim Right Action as the standard. Is it any wonder that regional meetings and the biennial gathering of delegates at General Synod end up with a divided house, satisfied winners and angry losers? The pastors, who themselves are spread out among the eight types, find themselves having to explain to their congregations why other congregations or the national offices could say or do things so contrary to the heritage of the church, as understood by each particular congregation.

Conversations with persons in other denominations reveal a similar spread of positions with the same consequence: polarization and rising anger. What this all means is that in these mainline churches a plurality of images, standards, and goals for the church has emerged. The dominant images of a denomination are easily identifiable, but other images find refuge and/or support in different settings of the church. Since few wish to acknowledge such radical pluralism, and most hope it will simply go away, there is little chance of mediation or resolution of such bitter conflict. The fact is that there is no process in place to resolve such substantive disagreement.

An appeal to theology to resolve the conflict is seldom helpful, because theology itself has been redefined as thought/action in the context of one of the competing interests. Instead of generating understanding and common ground, such discussions only generate frustration in the face of a chorus of competing words. This explains why so many complain that "no one is doing theology." What is meant is that no one accepts the norms that the speaker accepts for proper theological discussion. Lacking a common ethos and language, theological discussion becomes but another example of pluralism and ideological warfare.

Where theology descends into the polyphony of contending voices and slogans, churches turn to political and economic means to resolve disagreement. For some thirty years mainline churches have sought to resolve disagreement by parliamentary procedures and rules of order. Since the activist model demands that the church speak to all manner of social, political, economic, and moral issues, regional and national meetings have been preoccupied with resolutions. The short- and long-term consequence is ideological polarization. Parliamentary procedure operates on a binary system of either/or. Issues are decided either yes or no. People are either winners or losers. After twenty or thirty years of losing, the conservatives decided to organize and become as politically active as the liberals. Instead of creating new understanding or greater unity, the political model has only fractured the church. When it proves ineffective, individuals and congregations soon move to economic boycotts of programs, institutions, and parts of the church that do not appear in accord with their general and particular outlook.

A similar analysis can be made of a local congregation. Each church usually has a profile wherein one image of the church dominates, or perhaps two or three are joined together in a constellation forged by history and key personalities. At the same time all eight are probably present in the church, and the pastor, if he/she is theologically self-conscious, represents an individual profile. If the selection or appointment process was a good one, the pastor and congregation share a common image of the church, or they have identified this as a point of acceptable difference. If the selection process did not uncover the profile of the congregation or the pastor, then one is faced with a classic mismatch. Sooner or later someone will pay the price.

But consider church council debates when the eight views of the church collide. For example, how would one deal with admission of children to the Lord's Supper from the perspective of Sacramental Participation, True Faith, Right Action, Covenant Community, or World Unity? The approach to social issues would also vary considerably with each of the perspectives. In fact, how and why the church should even consider social issues would be affected by the eight views. Definitions of education (who teaches, what is taught, how it is taught, when and where) would likewise illustrate an interesting range of views if all eight models had their say. The role and authority of the pastor will obviously vary in the eight perspectives.

No matter what the tradition, American religion has been so affected by individual freedom that every congregation will have a large segment that is sympathetic to the image of the Covenant Community, that is, everything is a matter of individual conscience and freedom. The pluralism of the congregations also is increased by the addition of members not baptized and raised in that denomination. The entrance of former Roman Catholics into Protestant churches introduces a new set of dynamics into congregational life. In this situation, the one who must bear the burden of such pluralism, as well as the church fights, is the pastor. To the extent that his/her role is defined as holding things together, creating a positive attitude, or resolving all the issues, the pastor's role becomes precarious. In spite of all manner of social analysis demonstrating that what is happening in the congregation is the result of larger societal forces, the pastor too often feels it is his/her fault. But the problems are structural in nature and characterize most American churches. Even the typology of images of the church is only one factor dividing the congregations, as we have seen in Chapter One.

The Fullness of the Church

Having introduced this typology and its use, we can now draw several conclusions. The first is that each image affirms something valid and essential in the life of the church. This conclusion immediately sets us in opposition to the traditional logic of right versus wrong. Using such logic, one form is judged as authentic and all others wrong. Our approach moves in a different direction, seeking the positive image in each answer to the question of apostolicity.

A second conclusion is that while each image is valid, it cannot exist entirely by itself without severe limitations. The point here is not simply the specter of the negative development, for example, that Protestantism can become legalistic, doctrinal, or fundamentalist. Something positive is missing if one image exists without the other images. For example, without a rich sense of sacramental life and historical tradition, or the hope born of the Spirit, or the moral passion of Right Action, the classic Protestant theme of True Faith is fairly austere. Conversely, a sacramental tradition usually neglects strong, evangelical preaching. Or again, Pentecostalism and the Gathered Church traditions are short on a sense of history and ecumenical vision. The fact of the matter is that in most traditions the dominant form has been supplemented by the presence of several other forms, thereby limiting single-mindedness and enriching the life of the community. The best and most general example of this is the Catholic Church, which has always contained the model of True Faith as a counter voice to the model of Sacramental Participation in the Historical Community. It has been represented by priests, theologians, and religious orders, engaging and protesting the excesses of institutional power and authority. Moreover, the religious orders have embodied elements of the Covenant Community, Right Action, and the Pilgrim model. In Protestantism, the Great Awakening of the eighteenth century was in many respects a renewal that had strong elements of the image of Rebirth in the Spirit. Imagine what Calvinist scholastics thought of Gilbert Tennant, a Presbyterian, who preached a sermon entitled "The Danger of an Unconverted Ministry." While each form has demonstrated creative power to sustain itself in many forms of church life, each model has not been able to represent the fullness of Christianity by itself.

Third, the analysis also identifies how each form is corruptible. So much of church history involves the protest and warfare (real and spiritual) involving the negative developments of each image. In America many people have abandoned the churches because of the churches. In its negative forms, Christianity is its own worst enemy, driving people out. Even where churches sustain a positive form, the relation between churches is still influenced by the fear of the negative forms. But in spite of the corruptibility of each image, such developments do not invalidate the positive images. They only drive us to the paradoxical recognition that grace and sin, good and evil, are part of our religious experience.

Taken together, these conclusions allow us to see how the eight images complement one another. The challenge facing us is to explore ways that such diverse images of the church can be related in constructive ways. But how can this be done? The task is not simply one of seeking abstract formulae for assimilating the eight images. It would be somewhat irrelevant for someone to construct a theoretical solution. What is needed is a process in which individuals and groups can participate in the construction of church life that is more inclusive of all of the images. Such a process would begin with repentance for our all-too-frequent rejection of other images. To live in a time of ideological warfare means that few are willing to consider with genuine sympathy the images that inspire other forms of the church. The new absolutism of the left and right fosters both polarization and self-righteousness. Repentance means a break with such triumphalism and the recognition that we all have overstated our criticisms of one another. It also means the admission that we are all incomplete.

The next and more positive step would be to accept openly other images as valid forms of the church. There was a great breakthrough in Catholic and Protestant relations when Vatican II referred to Protestants as *separated brethren,* rather than *heretics.* Such irenic words of acceptance changed the relation between Christians and opened the way for honest speech and listening. In our time the practice of acceptance could begin with the exploration of how the images take form in the life of the individual and the group. What image or images are dominant in a congregation? Which do I fear or despise? What are the limitations of my own profile? How might I be enriched and grow by including other images into my life? The fact is that other images are already present in each person and certainly present in each congregation. Given the patterns of marriage and church membership, most Protestant congregations include former Catholics and a cross section of Protestants. Moreover, since some images appeal to certain personality types and/or stages of life, many people raised in their current denomination, with its dominant profile, are in fact living passively or actively in another profile. They no longer find their intellectual or spiritual needs met by the partial worldview of the dominant profile. In some cases they are actively living against it through negative behavior: nonattendance, nonsupport, opposition, or direct assault on the programs and pastor. Since we seldom talk substantive theology, the focuses of the disagreements are usually quite specific and in many cases trivial. It would be a wonderful event (taken in the literal sense of producing wonder) to give permission to each member of a church council to chart his/her personal profile. And of course it would also be terrifying. What if clergy did the same at the monthly ministerium? What if national leadership charted their profiles and attitudes toward the other images?

Honesty about our innermost commitments, in and of itself, will not create a new unity. Unity is the gift of the Spirit of Christ. Our hope ultimately is in the gospel, which transcends all eight of the models. The gospel can unite us and allow us to see how different traditions have faithfully embodied one or more aspects of it. But the peace of Christ also includes the challenge that each person see that he or she has only a part of the gospel and is in need of the help and enrichment that come from other parts. All must acknowledge that the true church is more complex and varied than we have imagined, and that it requires real integration of these ecclesial elements in actual ways. This is the hope for our ecclesial debate, but also the great challenge. The question is: In an ideological age such as ours, do we want to be reconciled, or would we rather hold fast to our partial views?

CHAPTER 3

The Signs of Our Times

To reform the church one must also speak of the world. This is not to suggest that the world must set the agenda or the standards — theological reform must proceed from the gospel. Rather, it is to be clear about the context of our discussion. Forces at work in the world — creative and destructive — are also at work in the church's people and its structures. They are signs of our times. How the church responds to these powers is decisive in many ways. Some responses are themselves points of contention: for example, consider the reactions to differing attitudes on abortion. Other responses are significant because they define the church to its members and to other Christian bodies: for example, attitudes toward war and peace. Even the silence of the church on such issues as sex, violence, and money is crucial because such a refusal to respond sends a clear message. As a community of the Spirit, the church needs to see the signs of our times. Such a reading is an act of spiritual discernment, whereby we acknowledge what is happening in us and to us, but also name its significance in light of the sovereignty of God and the grace revealed in Jesus Christ.

Discerning the Signs of the Times

What factors, trends, conditions, and powers of this world shall we name as the signs of our times? Here we shall focus on four signs of our times: difference, suffering, anger, and ideological warfare. All four are part of the church's life. How the church interprets and responds to them says much about the church's faith as well as the way the world has affected the church. But these four are chosen not simply because they are important trends in American culture. All four have an important thing in common: they have become ways in which people define themselves and their relation to other people. They thus have the potential, in their extreme form, of governing the way people name their identity and worth. As such, they rival and/or replace traditional Christian forms of identity.

To illustrate the point, we shall offer a play on words regarding a classic definition of humanity that has been handed down to us from the Enlightenment. When the philosopher René Descartes sought to reconstruct reality in the face of radical doubt, he began with human thought as the basis for self-understanding: "I think; therefore, I am." This affirmation was crucial for the Enlightenment because it defined human beings as rational creatures. But in our time human beings look to other human experiences to define themselves. We cannot fully understand the four signs of our times unless we see them as drastic revisions of Descartes's dictum, thereby redefining the nature of our lives.

I am different; therefore, I am.

The desire to be different arises from two sources. One is the drive for freedom, which is the dominant value in American society. Nowhere in the world has the freedom of the individual so marked a culture. Unencumbered by space and time, Amer-

62

icans have been free to live in new ways. This freedom also creates great expectations for individual self-determination. In traditional societies, one becomes a person by being like one's parents, ancestors, and mythic models. Work, class, marriage, residence, education, religion, family, and personal life are decisions determined by traditional practices. Hooked on freedom, American society places the burden for all of these decisions on the individual, assuming that freedom is best found in actualizing something new. Thus the drive to be different: one is truly a person when one breaks the bonds with one's parents and culture.

This is not to suggest that we live in a culture without traditions and social forces that channel or control decisions. There are such things as a dominant culture, mass media, corporate America, national systems of education, entertainment, sports, and religion. Parallel to the drive for individuality is the way a large percentage of the population opts out of freedom for the security of patterns, traditions, and conformity. Few persons are so independent that they can make all of life's decisions without reliance on other people and tradition. But the point is that conformity is not the first value in America. High-school graduates are not admonished to imitate their parents and preserve the status quo, but to actualize freedom, build a new society, and reaffirm values in a radically changing world.

In a culture marked by the phrase "Mother, I'd rather do it myself!" there will be continuous upheaval and change. Moreover, the demand for differentiation requires that whatever has been done to express freedom must be surpassed, or else one is simply accepting another's solution. Is it any wonder that we are faced with constant change, that moral and religious codes must be broken, that the extreme of last year must be surpassed this year? In such a society independence becomes a way of life. That there is tremendous conformity within subcultures and groups suggests that the ideal of absolute individuality may be unattainable. But such an observation is largely irrelevant in the face of the personal conviction that one has achieved one's own individuality by being different.

The second source for differentiation arises among people who are already different, but have not been recognized by the majority or included in the dominant value structure. If the dominant image of America has been shaped by the values of white, male Protestants living in traditional families in northern cities, most people do not fit such a model. In the last thirty years these people have served notice that they are different and that they exist. Their claim to difference is both a protest against exclusion and an affirmation of difference. By demanding that they be recognized in their particularity, they force the dominant culture to admit the pluralism of the society. That this pluralism has always been there is part of their protest. Thus for people of color, women, non-Protestants, gays/lesbians, people with disabilities, or divorced people to affirm their difference, two things have to happen: contemporary definitions of America need revision, but so do all the history books! Both our present and our past must be redefined in light of the fact that these differences have been and are now a part of this nation.

The resistance of the dominant culture to this protest/affirmation has produced much of the cultural warfare of the past thirty years. It has also made those claiming difference more resolute, refusing to back off in the face of resistance. Their goal has not been to become like the dominant group, but to achieve recognition as different alongside everyone else. For this reason distinctive marks of difference are emphasized with pride. Consider, for example, the willingness of African-Americans to be called black, or the credo "Black is beautiful." In a similar way women insist that there really is a difference in gender. Homosexuals declare that no apology is needed.

Subcultures refuse to be considered abnormal or deviant. If Jews and Catholics in the 1950s expected Protestants to admit that they existed, now Muslims, Buddhists, Hindus, as well other religious groups demand that Jews and Christians acknowledge their difference. And secular persons confront all religious people with the demand that they be acknowledged as persons of value. In one way or another, all of these persons and groups could no longer tolerate their exclusion, nor could they find freedom within the old dominant images that excluded them. It really is a different cultural world than that of 1960!

I suffer; therefore, I am.

Suffering dominates the lives of most people. But they do not readily identify with one another because the causes of their suffering are so varied and the reality of suffering is so personal. Consider the variety of suffering caused by the following:

- illness and death;
- personal stress, family problems, and divorce, finding expression in mental and physical illness;
- physical violence against individuals, from domestic abuse to random violence on the streets;
- natural catastrophes (floods, hurricanes, fires, earthquakes) and accidents (auto, ship, airplanes, industrial and environmental catastrophes);
- war, terrorism, and state persecutions.

This listing reminds us how many people are overwhelmed each day by the suffering caused by interpersonal problems, illness, violence, and large-scale catastrophes. Newspapers and television broadcasts have become a combination crime/war/ natural catastrophe report. In magnitude our century has produced overwhelming instances of suffering. No one event can claim preeminence because there are so many examples of human brutality. While the Jewish Holocaust is remembered in the West as the symbol of mass extermination and state terrorism, other instances of systematic violence dominate individual and social consciousness. In America, Native Americans recount a history of suffering covering four hundred years of European intrusion; African-Americans witness to a long history of slavery, segregation, and racism. In Latin America, liberation theology arises out of the suffering of the poor. In recent years, the intolerable brutality of civil war in Bosnia, Somalia, and Rwanda demonstrates that the will to harm has no bounds: rape, starvation, and slaughter have become strategies for social conflict.

Any list of examples is inadequate because it displays personal and hemispheric loyalties. The more we learn about world history in the twentieth century, the more instances of mass slaughter come to light. If modern warfare extended the concept of total war to include mass destruction of civilians, cities, and the earth, terrorism has perpetuated it as a regular means of political strategy. In its intensity and arbitrariness, it achieves its goal of evoking terror. Those who think they can escape this bombardment are still at the mercy of family and friends, who report their sufferings of accident, illness, and death. While we can protest that it is too much to endure, and observers note that it is a virtual overload that dulls our capacity for feeling, there is no escape. Some may achieve immunity, but most find that they are vulnerable.

The anxiety produced by this vulnerability is to a great degree magnified by the seeming arbitrariness of this suffering. It would appear that forces beyond our control are intervening into our lives in ways that are unpredictable. An auto accident, an instance of cancer, a plane crash, or a civil war bring suffering and death to persons without warning. Like Job, we feel that the severity of the suffering is completely out of balance with whatever faults we can acknowledge. Arthur McGill observed years ago that this perception of the unpredictability of suffering is fostered by the current journalistic style.[1] The news reports that a man standing on the street is shot or a family dies in an explosion. The implication is that one could be living a normal life and all of a sudden be killed. Violent forces suddenly intervene. McGill contrasted this style with journalism of a century ago, where there would be a deliberate attempt to place the event within a historical context, so that it was not unexpected. Our age, by contrast, has little interest in history or the long-term consequences of patterns of behavior. We have thus isolated the present, so that events appear as individual acts with no apparent reason. Thus a second pain is added to the suffering: the psychic terror that it is arbitrary and that we are victims of random violence and unnamed causes. Like the spokespeople for tobacco companies who see no connection between smoking and lung cancer, we see a world totally out of control, threatening us at every turn, for no reason at all.

Whether suffering is viewed as the result of random causes or deliberate acts, suffering evokes the perception that we are victims. The widespread use of the category *victim* and the creation of a technical term for this phenomenon (*victimization*) point to the way suffering has stamped our consciousness and behavior. It indicates that for many people, life has been changed (perhaps even transformed) by what was done to them. Whatever caution we might have regarding the overuse

---

1. Cf. Arthur C. McGill, *Suffering: A Test of Theological Method* (Philadelphia: Geneva Press, 1968), 28-31. While I was reading this book in 1976, the *Chicago Tribune* printed the headline from 1876 that announced Custer's defeat at the Battle of the Little Big Horn. The article began with a history of relations between Native Americans and the U.S. government, listing the violations of treaties and provocations that occurred in recent years. When one finally got to the description of the battle, the incident did not appear as a surprise, but as the inevitable outcome of the previous events.

of this vocabulary, the fact is that many people can rightly claim that their lives have been altered in ways beyond their control by individual or social action against them. Each year thousands mourn the loss of persons by accidental death and criminal acts. In this country alone, several million persons are directly related to persons killed in wars. Persons of color have endured social, political, and economic restrictions based on race. Women have lived with a double standard regarding gender in education, employment, and the legal system, as well as in the church. The more we are sensitive to issues of loss, grief, and social inequality, the more we become aware of how much suffering people endure.

This recognition creates a very complex situation. In major portions of the society, being a victim confers entitlement to government assistance and protection. In institutions such as the academy and the church, it conveys moral virtue and political power. One might even say that in these areas it has become so powerful that it represents a new form of moral currency. Those wishing to change the system or affect the agenda will have to relate to the politics of victimization. For if the major power groups claim authority and power because of their victimization, anyone seeking to share resources or time will have to deal in the currency of moral suffering. It is not surprising, therefore, that this has created a political upheaval. The traditional power structure of white men suddenly finds itself lacking the new moral currency. In a turning of the tables of power and privilege, white men find themselves lacking moral power, since they are not perceived as victims — in fact they usually are seen as the oppressors.[2] All of the arguments

2. While the attribution of most problems to white men may represent a liberation for some, it also generates new problems. The backlash of anger and resentment has become institutionalized in the politics of anger for the past twenty years. Following the elections of November 1994, reports began to

for quotas or broader representation in governance, for reme-dial programs or other changes, appeal in part or entirely to the history of exclusion and victimization.

This has opened the way for two dangers. One is that the claims to suffering will be abused and used for personal or political ends. In cases where those who suffer receive attention, care, special privilege, or benefits, the temptation is there to misuse such opportunities. This danger is very real in the church, which seeks to be gracious to people in need. What should the church do with those who assume the lifestyle of passivity and suffering? That they become quite proficient at using family, pastors, or kindly deacons (or seminary staff and faculty) is a common experience. Like the man at the gate of the temple in Acts 3, victims can become comfortable with their status. The thing this man least expects is for his situation to change. He asks Peter for money; he did not ask to be healed!

We have also seen the abuse of appeals to racism, sexism, poverty, physical disabilities, and emotional distress, as if every-thing were completely determined by forces affecting the in-dividual. This has created an extremely sensitive and potentially divisive situation within the life of churches and schools. On the one hand, there is a continual process of assessing needs, as communities practice the care and discipline of the Christian life. On the other hand, there are decisions to be made about membership on governing councils and boards, admission to seminary, grades, and readiness for ministry, in care status, and ordination, as well as selection of leaders for church and schools. What weight should be given to traditional expecta-

---

appear suggesting an increase in the number of white men voting for conser-vative candidates. But not all of the resentment is expressed openly, in political action or church discussions. In an institution like the church, where passive-aggressive behavior is well known, the anger and resentment beneath the surface continues to be a serious issue.

tions of the individual in contrast to claims of being a victim of physical or social forces? Are all of the traditional standards simply the expression of Western, white, male domination? If not all, which ones? The matter is quickly politicized, as people line up on opposite sides. At the heart of the issue is precisely the evaluation of suffering and the victimization it produces.

The second danger is that the overuse of victim language and frustration regarding the disputes just mentioned will cause us to become insensitive to the real suffering in our midst. This danger is probably more important and real. Racism, sexism, religious bigotry, discrimination toward homosexuals, and class prejudice are very real, and they do in fact cripple and destroy lives. The themes of vulnerability and suffering are not a passing fad or biennial study project. The church will need a theology that can deal with them in an honest and liberating way. Human suffering will not go away because we are weary of working on certain themes over time. People who suffer must not be at the mercy of our attention span, or even our frustration. If we are to talk about regeneration, it must include the regeneration of our capacity to see, to feel, and to show compassion toward the suffering of this world.

I am angry; therefore, I am.

In 1985 the faculty of Lancaster Seminary asked pastors, "What knowledge, skills and spiritual gifts will be needed in the next decade?" At the top of the list was the ability to deal with conflict. This response indicated widespread anger, as a dominant mood and source of behavior. While we were aware of what was happening in society, there was some surprise that the church mirrored society so exactly.

It is not difficult to understand how this could be. Our discussion of difference provides one explanation. The struggles for individuality — be it those expressing freedom in new ways

70

or those seeking recognition of their difference — bring with them anger and conflict. The more that families, institutions, or society in general refuse to recognize people, or perpetuate exclusion, the more anger finds expression in rebellion and violence.

The catalogue of sufferings presented above enumerates the ways people are violated. If suffering causes people to define themselves as victims, it also finds expression in anger. To be a victim is but half of a relation: sooner or later one concludes that this suffering has been caused by someone. Such a chain of logic is supported by the current legal advertisements, which set forth the position that if you suffer harm, it must be someone's fault (and they must pay). These advertisements encourage the already present link between victimization and vengeance.

Add to all of these causes the general feeling among so many people that things are falling apart: family life has gone sour, or even ended in divorce; one's expectations in work have not been realized; one feels betrayed by politicians or pastors; children have not met family expectations; illness has altered life and produced unbearable expenses; one's church is constantly changing; and most important, there is no recognition of one's own hurts or cause. All of this is happening in a culture dedicated to the pursuit of happiness.

The increase of anger, followed by conflict and violence, has meant that our domestic life mirrors our general society, while our neighborhoods mirror the strife of nations. Instead of the home being a safe haven and refuge from the world, we are faced with statistics charting the increase in divorce, the number of children raised by one or neither parent, and physical abuse directed toward women and children. Behind, with, and under these statistics is anger. Instead of being able to see our neighborhoods free from the hazards of terrifying international crises, the two begin to converge. The 1993–94 descriptions of Bosnia could also describe New York, Philadelphia, or Lancaster: racial and religious hatred; random shootings and bombings; rape and domestic violence; destruction of property; children living in terror, without food, clothing, or proper care. Behind, with, and under these descriptions is anger. Whether we speak of mass slaughter (as in Bosnia or Rwanda), terrorism, or celebrated murders, the world is dominated by anger finding expression in ill will and violence.

It is not extreme to say that in America anger, conflict, and violence have become a way of life. The patterns of behavior described by statistics suggest that anger is a dominant form of consciousness. Consider the turmoil in family life, the cold war in race relations, the tensions between genders, and the culture wars of the left and the right. In each of these areas there is anger directed toward someone. Newspapers and television dramatize the anger through the panels of political adversaries, which have become a form of political professional wrestling. The venting of anger and rage far outweighs the search for analysis or truth. Individual religious and political commentators discover that there is a large audience ready to express their anger. The radical right offers a litany of ancient grievances leading to a strong appeal to present fears and suspicion. The rhetoric is that of warfare: the other is the enemy; the strategy is that of spiritual and physical violence.

If anger and violence in the social-political realms were not enough, consider how violence dominates our entertainment. While football has always been a contest of physical strength, it has evolved into a use of force that reaches violent proportions. Fighting has become prevalent in professional hockey, basketball, and baseball. How is it that we seek out violence as entertainment: martial arts films, horror movies, espionage and detective stories, as well as films focusing on individual acts of violence? Is it just a matter of curiosity and the excitement of suspense? Or do we vicariously live out our own anger and thoughts of violence? Are we so angry that we would like to do these things to someone?

I oppose you; therefore, I am.

The social history of America since the 1950s involves an extended social conflict. It might even be appropriate to name this struggle as the second Civil War. As at the time of the first Civil War, our time is marked by fundamental divisions over values. We have witnessed the destruction of life and property. Moreover, there has been no official end: the passions and physical disruption of the '60s and '70s evolved into a seemingly permanent fracture between liberals and conservatives in the '80s and '90s. This split has institutionalized the expression of anger. The passage of time has not abated the passions because the issues have never been resolved. This was illustrated in 1994 in the aftermath of the death of President Nixon. The death of a president required recognition and comment from officials, the press, and commentators. But the comments only revealed the old divisions, as well as deep-seated anger and rage. It was as if nothing had changed since 1974, the year of his resignation.

James Davison Hunter has proposed that the ideological and social conflict of our time be understood as a culture war.[3] This image catches the imagination because it highlights two characteristics of this struggle. First, the struggle is ideological in nature, involving many different issues. Over time they create an interlocking network of values and causes. A culture war is

---

3. Cf. James Davison Hunter, *Culture Wars: The Struggle to Define America* (New York: Basic Books, 1991). The general idea of culture wars, involving multiple issues over time between two broadly defined worldviews, is drawn from this work by Hunter. I have developed this idea in a somewhat different way, and, as the reader will see, propose that Hunter relies too heavily on one central issue as the dividing point between the two cultures.

also fueled by the fact that we are loyal to family and friends, homeland, traditions, and social customs. In a culture war, issues have a history in which real and/or spiritual blood has been shed. There is a depth of feeling: anger, rage, and hatred toward the enemy and compassion and loyalty to one's own people. In ideological warfare one is defined by the remembrance of past wrongs as well as loyalty to present values. To call someone a northerner or a liberal, a redneck or a right-winger is to invoke a history of errors, violations, and evils. One knows who one is by who one opposes.

At the same time this polarization involves the structured relations of war. War is the ultimate form of polarization, involving enemies and strategies of destruction. Once war is declared, one lives within that framework. War allows one to accept the special arrangements and sacrifices needed, as well as the violence inflicted on both sides.

It is the combination of ideological or spiritual commitments with the structure of war that makes a culture war so destructive. The arrangements and practices of war, which loom so large in the midst of the fray, always rest on the ideological polarization that preceded them. In one sense all war is ideological in nature. War requires that conflicts be elevated to the highest level of value and incorporated into a worldwide context of good and evil, truth and falsehood. War is a conflict where the parties have concluded that no mediation or reconciliation is possible. The division of good versus evil is permanent. The particulars of actual conflicts are relevant, but fade in the glare of the bright lights of absolute judgments: Liberal! Radical Right! Communist! Black! Secular Humanist! Fascist! Ideological warfare can and does devolve into one-liners and slogans because particular analysis or argumentation has been replaced by broad spiritual or cultural commitments. Only on such terms can we accept the division and violence of warfare — be it spiritual or physical. All warfare must be preceded by a spiritual act of devaluing the other person. Ideological warfare is so important because it is the first step towards violence. In the name of what we deem right and good, people are driven to act against falsehood and evil. To observe that many conflicts involve polarities and half-truths does not lessen the intensity. People who are half right are very dangerous precisely because they do have some right on their side. In the name of their cause they are willing to do terrible things to those they deem in the wrong.

There is now no longer any doubt that a culture war is present and active in the church, be it congregational life or regional or national gatherings. The religious form of the culture war is one of the dominant forces in the church's life. It is intimately tied to the other signs of our times: the drive for individuality, the experience of suffering, and the presence of anger. One cannot attend a meeting without some aspect of the culture war emerging in the discussion. Like all warfare, it consumes immense amounts of time and energy. Careers are being altered or destroyed by the warfare.

Our purpose in examining the polarization within the church is twofold: to discover what substantive issues lie behind the ritual warfare; and to connect these issues with our general analysis of the church in Chapters One and Two. To this end we will analyze four issues that are central to the polarization within the church.

1. Authority

Hunter's thesis is that the two cultures, which he calls orthodoxy and progressivism, are divided over authority.[4] Orthodoxy defines it as absolute, fixed, and given, whereas progressivism is open to new ideas and an expanding view of authority. While the former looks to objectively given and transcendent authority, the latter looks to reason, experience,

4. Hunter, 31-51.

and personal freedom. Using this criterion, Hunter notes that the players in the new polarization are not different regions, parties, or churches, but the conservatives and liberals in all of these. Thus when conservatives argue against homosexuality, their number might include Jews, Catholics, and Protestants. They are united by an appeal to a fixed authority, that is, a tradition of interpretation regarding selected passages of Scripture. Those accepting the practice of homosexuality refuse to view the Bible in such a rigid way, appealing to linguistic, historical, and social factors.

Hunter is obviously correct that the two camps are divided by their approaches to authority. On an issue such as homosexuality, the split on authority appears crucial. But if one changes the issue, authority is not necessarily the point of division. For example, it will not explain why some conservatives will allow divorce, or modern dating of the earth, or usury, or military service. It is not possible to explain all of the conflict between liberals and conservatives by this one issue, or any single issue. There appears to be more of a constellation of values at work, connected over time in ways that will appear arbitrary to the other side. For this reason we include three other factors.[5]

2. Freedom

Both sides value freedom because it is the primary value in America, when compared to community, equality, or justice. But freedom has different connotations and is linked with different values on each side. Liberals define freedom as self-determination or self-expression, which make the individual the primary concern. Moving from one's own self-expression,

5. Since Hunter defines the culture war as competing moral visions or worldviews, there is obviously a recognition that many factors are at work. Compare, for example, his discussion of the way freedom and justice are viewed differently by the two camps (Hunter, 106-32). But even this discussion moves back to the discussion of different views of moral authority.

they are able to show concern for the self-expression of others. But the starting point is the self's liberty. A culture motivated by self-expression will over time be called permissive, valuing the free expression of individuals. This commitment to self-expression is evident in the liberal culture's view of sex: free choice and self-expression are values that take precedence over other values such as fidelity, family stability, parenthood, or general theories of human development and social order. Even an infectious disease crisis or an epidemic of teenage pregnancies seems not enough to question a view of sex based solely on self-expression.

By contrast conservatives tend to define freedom as the ability to maintain or contribute to the existing social order. The bias toward community over the individual is present here, as is the preference for the current social order, with its traditions and values. An example would be the tendency to endorse military service or war. Conservatives tend to endorse military life and action, but be outraged by the critics of such action. This endorsement extended through the Vietnam War and reappeared in the invasion of Iraq. But the radical support of conservatives for military action does not extend to the federal government per se. In fact, there is open hostility toward the government because of taxes, regulation, and perceived corruption. This suggests that the issue is not loyalty to the federal government per se, but maintenance of traditional values. Military service, national defense, honor, and personal valor are traditional ways in which one actualizes freedom because freedom is tied to the maintenance of tradition. If one begins from the opposite assumption, that freedom is self-expression, then participation in military service could be evaluated in different terms.[6]

6. In his commentary for the PBS television series *The Civil War*, the historian Shelby Foote remarked that while northern men could easily pay a person to take their place in the draft, such an option was out of the question for southern men because the women would not allow it. It was a matter of honor.

3. Sin

Both sides in the culture war make assumptions about what has gone wrong with individuals and society. It could be something that threatens one's physical life, a particular act, or an external force that is restrictive. In political terms the danger is called the enemy (e.g., Evil Empire); in religious terms it is called sin, evil, or the devil.

Liberals have always had difficulty with the view that the problem is in us, as Paul, Augustine, and Luther argued. Opposed to morbid talk about the sinful self and original sin, liberals tend to be optimistic about the self and affirm its goodness. To be sure, sin does take personal form in the liberal worldview, but it will not be described in Augustinian terms of excessive self-love or loving the wrong thing. It would be more common for liberals to speak of sin as the failure to actualize the self or acts based on ignorance. From such a starting point, one quickly moves to the external social forces that restrict or repress full self-actualization. This explains the liberal commitment to social programs designed to remove negative forces (e.g., eliminating racial discrimination in employment, or providing welfare as the means to give people sustenance and a second chance). The same merger of optimism regarding the self and pessimism regarding social forces appears in liberal attitudes toward sexual abuse: they are very concerned about the sexual abuse of women as a repressive social force, but they are somewhat silent about the origins of sexual abuse within the self. Words like *selfishness, lust,* or *covet* do not get much attention.

By contrast, conservatives have little trouble talking about sin and the threats of chaos and nihilism. The locus for such disorder, however, tends to be within the individual. Sin is the individual's fall from grace, or the inability to manifest moral standards and virtues. Since social order is the bulwark against individual sin and social chaos, it is difficult for conservatives to think of sin in social terms. Only if people are directly oppressed are conservatives able to imagine sin as oppressive economic, political, or social forces. Therefore the attention is given to sin as vices and foibles of the individual. But the back side of this view is to slam the door shut on any connection between individual actions and cultural influences. For example, conservatives tend to see murder as a deviate act by an individual, unrelated to a culture of violence. Or consider the reactions to the sexual misconduct of Jimmy Swaggart and Jim Bakker. These misdeeds are seen as individual acts — or even the work of the devil — rather than further evidence that some very negative and obsessive attitudes are at work in our culture. Whereas conservatives are horrified by such misdeeds because they threaten society with chaos, liberals are horrified because of the abuse to the individuals. The two groups may share the condemnation of a particular act, but for quite different reasons.

4. Salvation

Parallel to their views of sin, both camps have different approaches to salvation. Liberals tend to think of salvation in terms of personal happiness, with strong emphasis on self-expression and freedom from external repression. Conservatives tend to think of salvation in terms of empowerment to do the good, with strong emphasis on traditional community values. The good is defined in moral terms by rules that regulate and give shape and substance to life. Consider the importance of rules, discipline, formation, and practice among conservative Catholics, Protestants, and Jews. But the good can also be defined in terms of cultural goals: education, career, wealth, social status, power, or physical health. While liberals and conservatives will use a common language of salvation, peace, justice, and happiness, in reality the one thinks of these ideas in terms of the individual freedom, while the other sees the individual being formed according to traditional values.

What conclusions can we draw from this outline of divergences in the current culture war dividing America? First, it is clear that liberals and conservatives are divided by more than one issue, rather than solely by opposite views on authority. Liberals have created a culture that is governed by a constellation of values: self-expression, freedom from repression, an overriding fear of oppressive institutions, the inherent goodness of the self, and self-fulfilling activity that leads to happiness. By contrast conservatives tend to look to a different constellation of values: the maintenance of the existing social order, participation in community, a concern for order in the face of chaos, and life defined as the pursuit of the good.

The second theme that emerges from this analysis is that neither side is consistent in its use of these values. We are at a time when traditional definitions of *liberal* and *conservative* do not apply. For example, in theory liberals should be against regulation because it imposes restrictions by society on the free self; conservatives should be in favor of regulation because it provides a positive structure for individual life to develop while protecting the interests of the community. Consistent with this expectation, liberals are opposed to regulation of artistic expression and conservatives favor it. But liberals are in favor of regulation when applied to economics and the environment, while conservatives are opposed. Thus regulation is favored or opposed, depending on the issue.

Other examples can be explored that reveal how the constellation of values on each side shifts, depending on the issue. What this means is that each side is vulnerable to the charge of glorious inconsistencies. Take the example of the value of life. On abortion, conservatives abhor the destruction of the unborn fetus. In the name of the Bible and family norms, they are pro-life. Liberals reject these appeals in the name of the liberty of the individual, the overthrow of oppressive rules that force pregnant women to use self-destructive measures, or the problems cause by unwanted children.

But when the issue becomes that of the death penalty, the appeals to the sanctity of life are reversed. Conservatives favor the death penalty by appealing to the Bible, even though the appeal by Christians is to the Old Testament. Conservatives also appeal to arguments about deterrence, which is of interest because it is not supported by facts. One can only imagine that the argument of deterrence is a matter of belief, tied to the defense of the existing social order and the fear of chaos. Without the death penalty there would be moral chaos because murder would appear to go unpunished; without the death penalty there would be social chaos because violent crimes would increase. Against this sanction of state-sponsored death, liberals appeal to the sanctity of life, Jesus' teaching of non-vengeance and forgiving love, as well as the possibility of executing the wrong persons (which is the ultimate form of external repression against an individual).

What are we to make of this flip-flop? Both claim to be for life, but depending on the issue, the valuing of life takes radically different form. Both sides are vulnerable to charges of inconsistency, playing fast and loose with authority, facts, and figures. Only when you look at the configuration of multiple values do the positions become intelligible. But there is, of course, another factor: culture rivalry. Precisely because the other side — those people who have dumped on us time and time again — are opposed to what we want, we will stand firm for what we want no matter what.

A similar scenario emerges when we look at the issue of optimism regarding the individual. In theory the liberals are supposed to be optimists. They are notorious for their insistence that moral evil is embodied in social forces that repress the self. For example, the liberal view of sex affirms freedom and self-expression. Traditional conventions about sex before marriage, marital fidelity, or sex linked with genuine love are usually given secondary status to the value of the individual seeking authentic self-expression. The assumption appears to be an eternal optimism that individuals will be able to regulate their sexual activities in accord with the best long-term interests of their selves, their current family and friends, and the overall good of society. It is a position difficult to maintain, and leads to glaring inconsistencies.

Conservatives have always ridiculed liberals for their excessive optimism. Claiming to be closer to sacred texts, they have been bold to affirm the propensity of humans toward selfishness and the willingness to enslave themselves in compulsive behavior. But just when we are ready to take this as the last word, we find an outbreak of optimism among the conservatives. Consider the Reagan-Bush public relations campaign on drugs, wherein Nancy Reagan declares, "Just say no!" This declaration appeals to individual responsibility and indirectly affirms that the government cannot do everything — especially things relating to personal choice. But it also contains considerable optimism. In the face of intense pressure from peers in school and neighborhood, as well as heavy social and economic forces that push individuals toward using drugs and/or selling drugs, the government advises those so tempted to simply say no. This is hardly a Calvinist or Augustinian view of individuals caught in the grip of social forces, unable to save themselves except by a gracious intervention.

Another example of conservative optimism comes in the television advertisements by the National Rifle Association. The initial appeal is to the traditional hostility against Big Brother. "They" are trying to take away our constitutional rights. But then an unbelievable optimism emerges. The advertisement assumes that the individual, with rifles and shotguns in the closet, pistols at the bedside, and rapid-fire weapons in the footlockers, will be able to resist the temptation to use them. No matter what one's spouse says or does, no matter what the kids do, no matter how annoying the neighbors become, or how much the self is beset by fears, prejudices, anxieties, and fantasies, the self retains rational control. In the face of all of the provocations of modern society and the normal vicissitudes of life, the individual will show rational restraint. That is a very optimistic view of the individual. Even more surprising, there appears to be a convergence in the conservative view of guns and the liberal view of sex. In each case the argument is that the individual should have complete freedom. Perhaps it is best to let psychologists explain why the two camps converge on issues of sex and guns.

These examples illustrate how a culture war draws one into networks of logic and loyalty that are not always consistent and that lead to embarrassing contradictions. It would appear that we are moved as much by what we fear as by what we love. On some issues the operative values take one form, on others they shift precisely because other values are at stake. The one nonvariable is opposition to the other camp.

The Challenge to the Church

The argument of this chapter is that (1) forces at work in the world have changed the way many people define themselves and their relation to the world about them; (2) the presence of these self-definitions within the church during the past thirty years has been decisive for the internal life and agenda of the church; and (3) as definitions of human life they offer serious challenges to the Christian faith and community. The analysis of the four self-definitions has, it is hoped, made all three points clear. When persons are defined in terms of these four experiences, the faith and life of the Christian community will be challenged and changed. If human life is defined in terms of difference, in what sense are we united in Christ? If we are primarily victims, just what is our confession of God? If we are governed by anger and fully committed to the culture war, in what way are we part of the peace of Christ? To put the matter in terms of the language of faith, what will happen when people who define themselves by the four signs of our times are also asked to define themselves in terms of the answer in the Heidelberg Catechism:

QUESTION 1. *What is your only comfort, in life and in death?*

That I belong — body and soul, in life and in death — not to myself but to my faithful Savior, Jesus Christ, who at the cost of his own blood has fully paid for all my sins and has completely freed me from the dominion of the devil; that he protects me so well that without the will of my Father in heaven not a hair can fall from my head; indeed, that everything must fit his purpose for my salvation. Therefore, by his Holy Spirit, he also assures me of eternal life, and makes me wholeheartedly willing and ready from now on to live for him.

The discernment of these signs must be added to the analysis of the church contained in the first two chapters, which focused on the shape of religion in our society and the theological pluralism within the church. Yet even here the idea of adding a third set of factors is somewhat misleading. These forces cannot be added on as a separate list, alongside of the other two chapters. They need to be superimposed on the earlier discussions. They are not separate issues unrelated to the way religion takes form in our society or the battles over the nature of the church. They are part and parcel of the form and shape of American religion; they are directly related to why people have preferences for ecclesial models of the church. These forces are active in shaping the hearts and minds of people in the church. For example, when liberals opt for a view of the church as Right Action or the Liberationist model, they bring with them some or all of the agenda of the culture war. The same can be said for conservatives, who might opt for a Sacramental or Gathered Church model. Looking at the issues of differentiation or suffering reveals the same point: persons dominated by the drive for freedom are not going to be pre-occupied with the creation of community. In fact, they will probably react negatively to any use of communal language or any attempt to reaffirm our unity. Persons who come to seminary and ministry from the transforming experience of suffering will tend to incorporate that perspective in their view of ministry. This can move them either in the direction of personal healing and counseling or in the direction of social action directed toward eliminating the causes of suffering. Their experience not only defines them personally, but also defines the way they think theologically and sets the agenda for the church. We have, then, not a third issue, but a list of factors that enter in, with, and under all of the other cultural and theological issues we have already discussed in the first two chapters.

It must also be recognized that the four signs reviewed here are of a very mixed nature. They are not a list of four demons or idols of this world. The drive for differentiation can be a positive or negative force. Suffering is part of our human condition; how we deal with it can also change our lives. Anger is as much a positive reaction as it is a cause of problems. Ideological polarization cannot be easily catalogued. These four factors are named not because they share a common nature, but because they are the major factors defining people and the agenda of the church.

What are the challenges facing the reform of the church

85

from these signs, which have had such a profound impact on the life of the church? A general assessment is in order. Let us begin with the experience of suffering, since the subject of differentiation raises issues directly related to ideological warfare. The issue is more than whether the church is organized to minister to people in their need. To be sure, that is a major test for the mission and ministry of the church. But prior to that there are issues regarding our identity and the gospel itself. Will the church acknowledge the full reality and scope of human suffering in the world today? To do so would be to accept human vulnerability, weakness, and error. It is to admit, against the popular cults of youth and happiness, that not everyone is happy, healthy, or whole. Whether the church will name the multitude of sufferings present in its members and in the world becomes a crucial test of its willingness to be open and honest. To ignore this vast array of suffering in the hope that worship will be a happy hour is to ask most of the congregation to suspend their actual feelings. To ignore human suffering also separates us from the reality of the gospel, which is both radically honest and a message of hope.

To acknowledge suffering is not a matter of statistics; it is to admit that we ourselves suffer, that we are not always happy, healthy, or whole. In a society that lives with the idol of self-sufficiency and the goals of strength, independence, and success, such an admission is difficult. To suffer is to endure forces controlling one's life. It is to admit that we are not self-sufficient or in charge of our lives. That we resist such an admission is revealed in our reaction to the very title given to those who suffer. Persons admitted to hospitals are called *patients*. The word is derived from the root meaning "to suffer," which also gives us the words *passive* and *patience*. *Vulnerable* is derived from the verb meaning "to wound," and means "unprotected." All of these words bring us to the same point: in reality we are not very patient or passive, and we abhor being unprotected. Control, power, and self-determination are part of the American dream. In such a world, suffering is a physical and psychic threat.

Liberation theology, arising in the context of the suffering of the poor in South and Central America, has rightly placed God's concern for the poor at center stage. But in North America, where at least two-thirds of the people are not economically poor, we need to think of poverty in the broadest possible terms. This can and must be done without stripping the gospel of its concerns for justice or translating it into other-worldly piety.[7] Perhaps suffering is the key to opening the door to all people. If we understand suffering in the broadest possible way, it is possible to speak of God's concern for those who suffer. The suffering of most people is not visibly apparent, nor is it revealed in brief, perfunctory greetings. To be human is to suffer and be vulnerable, in spite of all of our protection and claims to security. Attending to suffering is always a matter of caring for other human beings. But it is also a matter of how we define ourselves and our power.

What then is the message of the church to those who suffer? Shall the church take up the cultural assumptions regarding suffering, which view it as a loss of identity and worth? Shall we endorse our abhorrence with suffering on the assump-

---

7. In his Introduction to the 15th Anniversary Edition of his famous work, Gustavo Gutiérrez makes it clear that liberation must be understood in a comprehensive way: liberation from social oppression; liberation of personal transformation; and the liberation from sin. Cf. Gustavo Gutiérrez, *A Theology of Liberation: History, Politics, and Salvation*, trans. and ed. Sister Caridad Inda and John Eagleson, rev. ed. (Maryknoll, NY: Orbis Books, 1988), xxxviii. If one takes seriously Gutiérrez's thesis that liberation theology is a theology of salvation for people in their history (Gutiérrez, xxxix), then it is consistent with his general theological orientation for North American Christians to ask about the multiple forms of oppression or poverty in addition to economic poverty.

tion that health and self-sufficiency are the sole marks of divine acceptance? And what shall the church make of those particular ailments that appear to arise quite directly from our overindulgence, the disrespect of our bodies, and the misuse of things around us? Shall the church accept the idea that such ailments are accidental and totally unpredictable, thereby joining in the conspiracy of avoidance and silence? In a world where more and more people awaken to the idea that things do not have to be this way, the church will need to be ready to listen and speak.

But perhaps the hardest challenge the church faces is the reality of human limits. Anyone who enters the world of suffering soon discovers that there are limits to our ability to heal hurts or resolve problems. For many who suffer, there is nothing we can do to make things right. We cannot bring back from the dead those destroyed by cancer or guns. No amount of anger or vengeance can bring them back to life. In the face of such limitations, what shall be the message of the church in an age that demands strategies for success? Is the church prepared to break with the cultural illusion of invulnerability and superficial happiness? It is sobering to recognize that there are times when the only thing we can do is acknowledge our limits and pray for a divine grace that will sustain us in the face of death. In a world where we are so deeply divided and have so little sense of a common life, suffering and the experience of powerlessness may be the narrow gate through which we must pass to rediscover our common humanity.

When we turn to anger and violence, we find another set of issues facing the church. The immediate one is obviously the presence of anger and conflict in the life of the church. But at deeper levels lie the experiences that produce anger and violence. The church cannot ignore these experiences, hoping that they will go away or that members will hold them separate from their participation in the life of the church. The experience of congregations and national church life has been that anger so repressed erupts sooner or later, and very often in unexpected ways.

The presence of anger in our society also has a significant impact on church growth. A church that does not speak honestly about what is happening to people, and at the same time offer some hope of healing, will appear largely irrelevant to the average person. Conversely, it is very tempting for churches to recruit people on the basis of their anger. By declaring that the church is against one issue, whether homosexuality, abortion, racism, sexism, violence, or any other single controversial issue, it is possible to rally people who are also against, and angry about, that issue. Or the unifying factor may be anger about measures that threaten a supported issue. The temptation in either case is to become single-issue churches, rallying people united in their anger. Such a strategy places the church in the middle of the culture war, with the church simply being another arm of ideological conflict.

In the face of so much anger in the society and church we might ask the seemingly absurd question: why would we want to increase the number of angry people in our churches by recruiting new members? After all, if conflict in the church is the dominant issue and new members are drawn from the same pool of angry Americans, will church growth only make things worst? Behind this absurd question lies a far more serious issue: how can we liberate people from the anger that has beset the culture and reconcile them to themselves and their neighbors?

Perhaps a first step would be to consider that people are so angry and prone to violence because they themselves feel violated. One thing we have not done very well is listen to their story. Can congregations be the place where people have opportunity to speak of the origins of their anger? Such an approach overthrows the imperial strategy of both the left and the right: that leaders will define the agenda, including what we should be angry about. But what would happen if we listened to people and allowed them to reveal how they saw their lives affected, threatened, and even violated?

To open such a door is of course frightening and very threatening. Will things get out of control? What if pastors and church councils cannot deal with the issues raised? What if everyone is angry about something different? These are fair and crucial questions. One could hardly pass through such a door without asking them or anticipating answers to them. But the fact is that in so many situations things have gotten out of control because the church refused to open this door. When things exploded, we were completely unprepared.

Several problems can be enumerated in anticipation of a more direct dealing with the reality of anger in our society. The first is that the church, as we have argued in Chapter One, has structured its life and language to deal with the individual, whereas so much of the anger present in our society deals with interpersonal and larger social problems. After years of focusing on religion as an individual matter, churches and members find themselves ill prepared to think about complex ethical and social problems.

Conversely, much of the actual practice in dealing with the social agenda of the past thirty years has borrowed the language of social and political analysis. Issues have been framed in terms of oppression and liberation. This relies heavily on an analysis of power: who has power and who is powerless? Who is being oppressed? How can powerless people get power to change their situation? While such analysis is absolutely relevant in dealing with social conflict, it leaves open a set of issues.

(1) A power analysis is usually quite clear about the current inequity, but it is less clear about a vision of a new heaven and earth. While it is strong in identifying repressive forces, it

seldom makes clear how the two sides are to be ultimately reconciled. At its best, it points the way to changing the balance of power.

(2) Without a transcendent vision, power analysis must rely on guilt and fear to motivate people. How much of the anger of militants arises from personal guilt, seeking self-purification as much as the improvement of the social situation? When our need to do something is an expression of our guilt, discussions about strategy for social change are compromised. We are not speaking objectively about what will actually improve the situation, but about our own needs.

(3) Conversely, the reliance on guilt has reached a point of saturation. A culture caught up in the midst of thirty years of power analysis now is virtually immune to charges of responsibility. In fact, large segments tend to react just the opposite: power analysis only prompts people to get angry rather than feel guilty.

(4) Power analysis is appropriate in dealing with oppressive relations between people. But it does not deal very well with the anger and violence arising within the individual. Here the silence of the liberal tradition regarding sin as ill will and selfishness within the individual, and the bias in favor of sin as external forces, makes us unprepared to deal with the situation. Are we prepared to speak of the ways human life is deformed by virtue of our self-love, as well as by social forces?

(5) Finally, power analysis raises the hope that things can change. In most situations they can be changed for the good. But in many situations things will not change, and there is little we can do. What is the message of the church when we cannot fix things?

To criticize the limits of strategies based on political realism is not to deny their usefulness in specific contexts. It is to ask whether the gospel has anything to say to afflicted and angry people other than a call to power politics. Shall our appeal be basically one directed to guilt and fear? If we believe that neither the law nor worldly power can resolve in any final sense the conflicts of this world, then our theology will have to reflect the larger vision of the gospel. What is to liberate the nations of the world from the perpetual cycle of warfare? And who shall liberate us as persons from our own anger and alienation? If our anger will not be removed by getting even — because that is not possible — how shall it be removed? Are we not led again to consider that Lamb of God who takes away the sins of the world by removing his entitlement to revenge?

Finally, we come to issues raised by the drive for differentiation and ideological warfare. To begin with, the drive for differentiation calls the church to support the freedom of persons. As Paul Tillich argued years ago, the church must always side with causes of liberation over against repressive or exclusive forces. It is clear that repression by the majority has marked our culture and the church for centuries. Against such the church must be a refuge and an ally. The more the church positions itself in support of freedom, however, the more it faces a difficult balancing act: How can the church affirm the freedom for differentiation and at the same time affirm that we are members of a common humanity and nation? The excesses of freedom are overwhelmingly evident in American society. To state the question in the extreme: Can the church endorse the illusory goal of finding one's identity in total differentiation and at the same time talk a language of heritage, tradition, and community?

To illustrate the tension, consider several ways the drive for individuality impacts the society and the church. First, in the current church climate, the affirmation of particularity has left far behind any appreciation of commonalities. A whole generation of leaders view individuality and plurality as positive, while unity and commonality are viewed as negatives. The mere mention of unity and common life evokes an instant rejoinder that one is not appreciating the virtues of freedom and pluralism. On these terms the alternative to pluralism is repressive uniformity. Forbidden to speak of common ground, we are left wondering whether it even exists.

Second, with the collapse of an overarching vision of unity, based on common values, we are ushered into a cold war between major groups. Race relations deteriorate in the face of frustration regarding old federal programs, the increase in violence and hate crimes, and the absence of a positive vision for the future. Gender relations also lack a clear vision of how men and women can overcome the history of inequality and abuse without simply portraying men as the villains. It is striking that in matters of both race and gender, language symbolizes the impasse: how do we talk to one another in a situation where everything can be an opportunity for offense? How fitting that the popular book on gender relations should have the title *You Just Don't Understand.*[8]

Third, we appear to be moving more and more toward partition of the society by race, gender, class, ethnicity, religion, sexual orientation, and culture. This of course is not new in America or abroad. On the international level, partition has been used to divide Germany, Ireland, Vietnam, Korea, Bosnia, and the Middle East. The American church has been partitioned for centuries by race and ethnicity. It now appears to be dividing according to theological and cultural values. In all of these cases the underlying assumption is that differences are irreconcilable. When this assumption is joined with a moral evaluation, one is then faced with the partition of good and evil. Those who claim to understand spiritual matters need remember that acts of violence — terrorism or official warfare — must always be preceded by a spiritual act of devaluing the other side. The

8. Cf. Deborah Tannen, *You Just Don't Understand* (New York: Morrow, 1990).

different becomes the opponent; the opponent becomes the enemy. And ultimately the enemy becomes evil, worthy of death.

The solution of partition brings us face to face with the challenge of ideological polarization. As the culture war has developed in the church, both left and right have made it clear that each seeks to establish a test for entrance into the church, according to their agenda. Both sides claim divine approval for their theology and agenda, and wish to impose it on everyone else. Each side would sooner destroy the church than accept any mediation or reconciliation with the other. To say that the culture war of left and right is a dead end and counterproductive is a correct but incomplete assessment. We must also say that the culture war is an end to the church and a repudiation of the gospel.

At the heart of the conflicts within the church and the society is the simple question: what is the basis of union between any two people? What unites a parent and child, a man and a woman, siblings, persons of different races, classes, or religions? The dominant answer of ideological warfare is "You must be like us." That this is impossible or that it leads to endless bloodshed in this country and throughout the world does not appear to detract from its support. At every level of the church, amid all the rhetoric and conflict, the question is, is there a basis of union in the face of radical difference? The answer of the gospel is clear. But we resist it, preferring to continue the war.

CHAPTER 4

The Gospel of Reconciliation

A Parable

There once were a man and a woman who lived in a tree. They liked living in this tree, in spite of the obvious restrictions. In the tree they found shelter, a view of the world, fruit for food, and even branches to climb for exercise. Friends and family came to visit them in the tree. The fruit of the tree was exchanged for other needed goods. There came a time, however, when their children announced that they wanted to leave the tree. One son said that he wanted to see the world — the mountains and lakes, the cities and faraway regions. The parents said they too longed to do this, but could not bring themselves to leave the tree. So the son left his parents in the tree. The other child said he, too, wished to leave, since he found life in this tree quite restrictive. The parents could not understand this, and asked if he simply wanted to have his own tree. The son said yes, that was the basic reason for leaving. As years passed the parents found fewer and fewer people visiting them in their tree. They devised ways to try to bring people to their tree: They held certain festivals where they gave away the fruit of the tree. This worked for short periods of time, but other times it was very lonely. So they tried to make their friends feel guilty about not visiting them in the tree. This only caused people to stay away. Then they thought they would threaten people: they would throw branches down on people if they did not come to their tree. But this was not successful, since people only walked wider circles around the tree. Life became more and more frustrating, as they could not meet their needs nor could they spend much time with other people. So their life came to a close. They tried every manner of strategy to solve their needs, except for one: it never occurred to them to come down from the tree.

If the church is to be renewed, it must undergo reform by means of the gospel. It has tried all manner of strategies dealing with program and organizational analysis, church growth, and fund raising. No matter how badly these efforts fail, it is reluctant to turn to its own priceless treasure. For the gospel is, after all, no simple remedy that can be controlled by individual interests or ecclesial agenda. It is the power of God for salvation, an encounter with the living God who will change things, as promised, only according to a divine will quite contrary to ours.

It is the thesis of this essay that reform of the church must be theological, that is, be grounded in the hearing of and reliance on the gospel. Theology begins with critical reflection on the church and world in light of that gospel, and moves toward a confession of the gospel for and against the church and the world. Theological reflection and confession cannot produce reform or renewal; but they can turn our attention to the church's true treasure.

Starting Again: The Cross of Jesus Christ

Let us begin with Paul's elaborate and profound uncovering of the significance of Jesus in 1 Corinthians 1–2. The Corinthian crisis is well known and parallel to ours. The church is divided into several camps along theological and moral lines. There are competing claims to authority based on superior knowledge or spirituality. There are some disruptive moral practices, which suggest some see themselves as free from conventional rules because they are above the law. The community is thus threatened by rivalry, boasting, contentiousness, and varying levels of anger. When Paul says that he has heard from Chloe's people that there are quarrels among them, he is showing remarkable understatement. Having already written them once, he now writes again.

After greetings and thanksgiving in the name of Jesus Christ, Paul goes directly to the divisions in this church. But then he suddenly changes course. Having opened the matter of their strife, Paul does not proceed to chastise them or to give practical advice, pending his next visit. Instead he introduces the subject of the cross. The argument is strategically brilliant. One might even describe its design as a rhetorical trap. But if it is designed to catch the Corinthians, its ultimate purpose is to reveal the power of salvation.

Paul suggests that the crucifixion of Jesus represents the struggle between the world and God. The terms of the struggle are wisdom and power. The world, in its wisdom and with its power, rejected Jesus. Religious authorities considered him a blasphemer and iconoclast; political authorities saw him as a threat to their authority and the status quo. The key for Paul is that Jesus was rejected and put to death by institutional authorities committed to maintaining honored traditions. These were the very values that undergirded the current order. Jesus was not killed by thieves and gangsters, terrorists, or even random violence. He was put to death in accordance with claims to wisdom and power, on which the world relies for its survival. The initial outcome of this struggle portrays the wisdom and power of the world against the abandonment (folly) and death (weakness) of Jesus on the cross. Jesus' resurrection, however, turns everything upside down. For if God has now raised the crucified one to be Lord, then the initial foolishness of Jesus' suffering and the weakness of his death are transformed. On these terms, God's foolishness and weakness turn out to be wiser and stronger than the wisdom and power of the world. But even more is revealed: it is not simply that God's wisdom and power are greater than the world's. What is now revealed is that the world's wisdom is not wise at all, since it did not know God's plan. The world's power is counterproductive, since it was supposed to create life but only produced death. For Paul, the cross is the unveiling of the world's failure to know God and use power to achieve the very thing it espouses: life, justice, and peace.

The argument presented in 1:18-31 is designed to evoke from the Corinthians a new answer to the question, who killed Jesus? The simple answer, and the one every confirmand knows, is the Jews and Romans. Paul, however, has reframed the question in such a way that the standard answer is irrelevant. The answer Paul draws from the struggle between the world and God is this: Jesus was crucified by those making claims to wisdom and power. Here is the trap for the readers at Corinth. Their entire life consists of claiming moral and spiritual wisdom and power. If Jesus was crucified by people making claims, then the Corinthians have repeated this action, only in this case the violence is directed toward one another.

What we have, then, is an argument that has affected every generation of Christians since Paul because of its universal application. Paul drafts a response to a specific situation, which history would have easily forgotten. In the process he elevates the terms of the discussion above personalities and relative details to make his case. In its simplest form, Paul is arguing that two things follow from belief that Jesus is Lord. First, it means an end to ultimate claims based on our wisdom and power. The cross reveals what happens when we claim too much for our knowledge and ability to create just systems. Overcommitted to claims, our causes become crusades and our moral standards become oppressive. As Reinhold Niebuhr never tired of pointing out, there never has been a war where the participants did not claim it was fought in self-defense or in defense of universal values. Classes, ethnic groups, nation states, and grand alliances engage in competition and coercion in the name of their claims. Religion has not been exempt, but tempted more than the rest because its claims are sacred, evoking from its followers a devotion justified by appeals to God. It is the failure of such ultimate claims that reveals their idolatrous character. In practical terms, an idol is that which cannot produce what it promises. Time and again we have overcommitted ourselves to our claims in the name of the most noble virtues, only to find that far less was accomplished, with some cases producing only great suffering and evil.

If Paul appears to be engaging in deconstruction (i.e., a rejection of all systems and structures because of their corruptibility), we need to remember that he is in the tradition of the Mosaic covenant, wherein God will not be contained in human forms (be it magic or religious traditions), as well as the prophets, who have much to say about the difference between the ways of God and humans. Jesus certainly displayed the ability to discern the way religious and political institutions lose sight of their original intent and become ends in themselves. What Paul reminds the Corinthians, and every other reader, is that if the world in its power and wisdom does not know God and the messengers of God, then there is something wrong with the world. The sign of this error is the crucifixion of Jesus, but also the crucifixion of the innocent in every time and place.

That the innocent (the poor, the victims of religious and racial hatred, the peoples living under tyrannical systems) should suffer and die by deliberate design or benign neglect reveals the moral evil present in the world.[1]

The application of this radical judgment against the world is unrelenting and total. Here we need to return from its universal application to the specifics of Corinth. 1 Corinthians 1:26-29 is unmercifully blunt:

> For consider your call, brethren: not many of you were wise according to worldly standards, not many were powerful, not many were of noble birth; but God chose what is foolish in the world to shame the wise, God chose what is weak in the world to shame the strong. God chose what is low and despised in the world, even things that are not, to bring to nothing things that are, so that no human being might boast in the presence of God.

Whatever their claims, in fact they do not amount to much. In

1. It cannot be underscored enough that this reading of Paul, which I take to be his intent, is not an anti-Semitic interpretation. From Paul's perspective, the opponents of Jesus are not an ethnic or national group per se, but human beings engaging in ultimate claims. It is of course a source of great anguish for Paul that the leaders of Israel rejected Jesus and the early followers. But as he emphatically states in Romans 11, God has not rejected Israel. This places Jews and Christians in a precarious situation, since from Paul's perspective, both are claimed by God but each makes opposite claims about Jesus. From this perspective, Christians will never overcome their anti-Semitism unless they can accept their rejection by this people so loved by God. Much of the discussion about a cessation of anti-Semitism approaches the issue from the view of a denunciation of the violence against Jews, which is obviously a correct judgment. But what is discussed less is the fact that the two sides disagree on the most fundamental thing: whether Jesus is the Christ. Is it possible for Christians to recognize this disagreement and draw a conclusion other than anger and violence? On this very point Paul, the former zealot, may give us the answer: even the most radical disagreement must be acknowledged and placed before God, in the confidence that it will be resolved in the mysterious plan of God.

the new covenant community, no one may assert higher status or special privilege based on human claims. Paul is proposing that the Christian live without claims. But even more, he is denouncing every act of claiming as a form of violence (crucifixion) against one's brother or sister. Since these are brothers and sisters in Christ, the violence is also against Christ.

This brings us to the second aspect of believing that Jesus is Lord. Paul launched into a critique of all divisive claims because they are destructive and in the end idolatrous. That side of his argument is but the prelude for the positive side: saving wisdom and power are revealed in the crucified. They are received not by claims to human wisdom and power, but by trust in God. The true wisdom and power that lead to life rather than death are a gift. In the end it is a matter of grace.

That salvation is a gift is the foundation of all of Paul's thinking. Whatever meaning is given to salvation (i.e., forgiveness of sins, standing before God, freedom from destructive powers, personal worth and well-being, reunion with other persons, new life, the ability to love), such a development is not a human achievement or a reward conferred on those with special status. It is a gift. This was central to Paul's own conversion experience and became the governing image for interpreting the gospel. For example, in Romans Paul makes the point all the more explicit when he declares that the righteousness of God is revealed in Jesus (1:16-18). The choice of the word *righteousness* is the key. In traditional terms, mercy and love are usually contrasted with holiness and righteousness. From this perspective one can ask, how can a holy God be merciful? If God loves the sinner, is God righteous? By declaring that the righteousness of God is revealed in the suffering, death, and resurrection of Jesus, Paul cuts through all such dichotomies attributed to God or found in our concepts. It is the nature of God — as holy and merciful, righteous and loving — to bestow new life. Grace is an act of holiness to reclaim and restore the creation; it is an act of love to overcome the alienation between the world and God. Grace possesses all the power of love and holiness, united to overcome evil with good. The gift of righteousness thus governs the relation between the world and God. On the one hand, God cannot tolerate anything other than righteousness. The holy God will oppose all that destroys the life and goodness of the creation. On the other hand, God will not allow the earth to perish. Salvation is a testimony to the divine faithfulness. By declaring that the righteousness of God is revealed in Jesus Christ, Paul rejects the equation of righteousness with a judgmental moralism, which can end only in vengeance.

The mystery of this revelation is not simply that it is revealed in the crucified. The mystery is also present in our relation to it, namely, that it is received with a repentant and trusting heart rather than as a result of human achievement and enterprise. For Paul the cross always has this double message: (1) It is a *judgment* against every claim to superior knowledge and every form of moralism and legalism. Before the cross, we are left without any claim to such righteousness. (2) This judgment is ultimately not destructive but life giving. It clears away ever possible relation that we might have to God, other than one: the righteousness of God can be received only as a *gift*. One's identity and worth are given by God; one is a son or daughter (rather than a stranger or slave) of God, free to live in the knowledge that one's standing before God is bound to the gracious promise revealed in Christ. This freedom represents the liberation from the tyranny of all worldly claims, which intimidate the soul with guilt and fear. As Jesus observed, anxiety about the morrow is part of the daily life of humankind. Only the gracious word of acceptance from God can put us at rest. Moreover, only the person secure in personal worth is free to love, share, and be merciful. In a competitive world, where one must continually strive to protect oneself or gain advantage for the morrow, who can afford to divert attention from oneself to care for others? At best, one can participate in what modern society calls charity — a most inappropriate use of the word, since it has come to mean donations given from surplus in the face of emotional appeals.

This reference to the ability to love makes clear that for Paul there is a straight line between the gracious action of God in the cross and the being and doing of a Christian. The Christian life is totally formed by the gracious action of God, creating a new reality. Paul must create a new language to describe it: the new humanity, being in Christ, being in the Spirit, the body of Christ, and having the mind of Christ. There is a new being grounded in the new reality of Christ, from which new doing is both possible and expected.

At this point we need to speak to two objections against this reading of Paul. The first objection is this: if Paul asks the Corinthians to give up their claims to knowledge and power, how is it that he is allowed to make his claim? If all claims are to be given up, why should Paul have the last word? The fact is that Paul does make one claim, which he believes takes precedence over all others. That one claim is that salvation is a gift of the gracious God. Paul justifies this claim by two appeals: (1) the appeal to his own encounter with Jesus, crucified and raised from the dead; (2) the appeal to its consequences. Corinth is in a state of division and strife. Such is the natural outcome of the multiple claims. Only the single claim of the gospel, by contrast, is able to produce unity and peace, because it alone is inclusive and life giving. This double appeal is really all that we can ever make: on the one hand appealing to God and the tradition that interprets God's revelation, and on the other hand appealing to the consequences that flow from it.

From our vantage point we can test Paul's claim with a similar double appeal. We can appeal to the tradition surrounding Jesus. We do not know in what form Paul received the tradition. But Paul's central claim is both consistent with the written Gospels that we have and goes directly to the heart of Jesus' very own teaching. Jesus' teaching and parables about the coming rule of God, as well as his direct admonitions to the disciples about love and service, affirm that we are called to a radical trust in God and not ourselves. Time and again Jesus affirms that life itself, as well as forgiving grace, are gifts from God. We can also test Paul's prescription for Corinth against our own experience. Multiple claims to knowledge and power lead to division and conflict. They are usually resolved in this world by power, or go unresolved by the acceptance of permanent division. A realistic reading of the human situation inevitably ends with the question, is there a word that transcends all of the words, that is inclusive and liberating? Such a test must be used to evaluate Paul's message as well as any application of the Corinthian argument, including this one.

The second objection has to do with the proposal that Christians are called to live without claims. Paul has in effect stripped the Corinthians of their claims. Persons appealing to achievements and virtues are suddenly left without status. For many in our times, imbued with perspectives drawn from the social sciences, Paul appears to be advocating a kind of psychic self-destruction. Others will simply take this reading of Paul as confirmation that Pauline Christianity is indeed negative and repressive.

Let us respond by affirming that in our view, Paul's concern is not to question what we today would call positive human development, that is, the ability to affirm oneself in and among other persons, based on self-confidence and self-esteem.[2] In-

---

2. There is, of course, the set of verses in Paul's letters that clearly argue for subordination of women to men, which are usually taken as evidence that Paul does have a flawed anthropology. I take these verses as evidence that Paul is thoroughly immersed in the social conventions of his culture, but that they

tellectual development, emotional stability, and practical competence are all aspects of normal human development. Paul's concern is that the process of normal human development takes place in a world dominated by self-interest and division. In such a world it is difficult to find normal development, that is, development unaffected by selfishness, competition, anxiety, and division. In a society that expects individuals to create their identity and worth by their achievements and possessions, within a social context of competing pressures and values, all activities are open to misuse. Our anxiety regarding goodness, knowledge, and power tempts us to invest things in this world with more value than they can bear. In effect, we invest absolute value in the relative things given to us for our use and enjoyment. Work, education, family status, friends, personal achievements, and wealth become absolutes that guarantee worth and well-being. None of these things in and of itself negates trust in God. But in biblical terms, sin is the self-love that turns us away from God to self-centeredness. It involves the misuse of our minds and bodies, our achievements, and all the things around us. When identity and worth are ultimately defined by these things, then the normal claims of life become ultimate claims. When this occurs, they are idols that do negate our

---

contradict his essential message that in Christ there is neither Jew nor Gentile, slave nor free, male nor female. Like most of us, Paul is not consistent; he is still in the process of understanding the full implications of the very gospel that he proclaims. Such an interpretation will not sit well with literalists, who claim both views of Paul as binding, but seldom tell us how they are to be reconciled. Such a direct approach is not opposed to the attempt that wishes to soften Paul's references to women by alternate meanings drawn from linguistic or historical studies. But such studies change. I would prefer to deal with these verses by means of the theological standard Paul himself establishes: the unity of Christians established by the grace of God in Christ. Such a theological approach also makes it clear how we should deal with Paul's toleration of slavery in Philemon.

trust in God. No sooner has trust turned from God than it also turns from other people and the earth. The self that has invested its absolute love and trust in itself or its societal claims will be abusive of other persons and cultures.

If an example is needed, we may consider the difference between normal relations of intimacy and destructive ones. In normal or healthy relations of intimacy, be it the relations of friends, siblings, or married persons, there is a sharing of thoughts and feelings, degrees of personal disclosure as well as nurture and support. As persons reveal more of themselves and engage in greater degrees of trust, there is a corresponding expectation of trust and fidelity from the other. Friendship, family life, and marriage hold in a delicate balance the giving of trust and the expectation of trust. In destructive relationships, by contrast, this mutuality of trust is broken. The abusive person defines the other person as an object, to be used and manipulated. Self-centered persons are abusive in friendship or romantic love because the other person is defined in terms of the self-centered one's interests. The reference to *being used* is quite accurate in describing destructive relationships. In biblical terms such abusive relationships represent the idolatry of one party defining itself as ultimate and the other as subordinate. Such pretension inevitably produces alienation from God and other people, since neither God nor other people can tolerate for long such idolatrous claims.

The proposal that we live without ultimate claims, therefore, has to do with the misuse of our talents and achievements, or, as Paul says, our wisdom and power. It has to do with living without making ourselves the center of the world. This brings us back to the problem Paul has with boasting. Such an act signals the presence of pride and self-centeredness, allowing the person to set himself or herself above others. One cannot speak of boasting without immediately recognizing the twofold dimension of this act: the effect on the one that boasts and the effect on relations with other persons. When one crosses the line from a joyous celebration of the goodness of life to making one's achievements the basis for one's life, one instantly transforms oneself and one's relations to others. There can be no ultimate claim except that of God, no boasting except that of God's gift in Jesus Christ.

The Gospel of Reconciliation

The analysis of 1 Corinthians 1–2 reveals all of the components of a theory of atonement. The central agent is God, active in and through Jesus Christ. The antagonist is the world. The issue is the nature of true wisdom and power. The key event is the cross, which precipitates a crisis of trust. The cross simultaneously unveils the futility of the world's claims and reveals the saving power of God. This double disclosure culminates in a choice the hearers must make: to persist in trusting the world's claims, even in a revised and hopefully improved form, or to give up all ultimate claims but for one, namely, that identity and worth are gifts of God. These gifts are received only through repentance and trust of the heart, issuing in faith, hope, and love. The removal of the world's claims, which are the source of endless division and warfare, opens the way for a new reality: the reconciliation of human beings with one another and with God.

From this perspective we are warranted in suggesting that 1 Corinthians 1–2 presents a fully developed interpretation of Jesus' death and resurrection, and not simply a brilliant but isolated play on the words *wisdom* and *power.* If this is correct, two conclusions must be drawn. First, this interpretation is significantly different from others in the Pauline writings. The central issue of crisis in the face of ideological conflict, leading to reconciliation, is not the primary issue in other passages, which have become the basis for theories of atonement. In Romans Paul introduces the legal or juridical image, with sin incurring the judgment of the law. There the issue is how sinful beings can be reconciled to a righteous God. The argument in Galatians again revolves around the tensions of the bondage of the law and the freedom of the gospel, as well as the contrast between works and faith. To be sure, Galatians affirms the unity of believers, against the divisions of humanity (i.e., Jew/Greek, slave/free, male/female: cf. Gal. 3:28-29). This theme is more fully developed in Ephesians, with the image of the breaking of the dividing wall. But in both Galatians and Ephesians, the primary division is that of Jew and Gentile, stemming from the centrality of the law. In Philippians the self-emptying of the divine agent of God is presented as both an interpretation of the cross and an image for humanity (cf. "Have this mind among yourselves . . . ," Phil. 2:5). In several places the power of God over sin, death, and Satan is boldly presented, laying the way for more fully developed theories of God's conquest over demonic powers. But in none of these interpretations is the source of hostility between human beings or between God and the world defined as ultimate claims to wisdom and power. By dealing directly with a case of spiritual warfare, Paul goes beyond the language of works/faith, law/gospel, which has been the language of the dominant theories of atonement. First Corinthians 1–2 does not require us to apply, by intermediate steps, the affirmations of grace and freedom from the law to ideological divisions. Such divisions are the primary issue. The power of salvation is revealed in the face of hostility based on our world's claims to truth and power. The gospel of reconciliation is thereby expanded for Paul and the Corinthians, as well as for us.

The second conclusion is that in 1 Corinthians 1–2 we have the basic elements for a theory of atonement that is also distinct from the other classic theories. Paul has given us an approach to the significance of Christ that we shall call the *crisis-reconciliation* motif. By analyzing the major aspects of this view, in relation to other theories, we will demonstrate why it points to the power of the gospel for our time. While we shall not argue that this motif is superior to others, since they deal with different issues, it can be suggested that this motif has the potential of incorporating the others in a comprehensive perspective. The comparison of this view with other atonement theories is also relevant because of the impact of such theories on the view of the church. The history of Christianity reveals direct correlations between understandings of the work of Christ and views of the nature of the church. For example, when the medieval church is considered to be a spiritual reality different from the secular world, it usually relies on the affirmations of the incarnation in Athanasius as well as the conquest of Satan in Irenaeus. The focus on the authority of the church as the means of grace can be linked to Anselm and all others who perceive the saving power of the divine-human Christ mediated to humanity through the sacraments. In Protestantism, if the work of Christ is understood through legal motifs (i.e., sin as a violation of the law, Jesus fulfilling the law by dying in our place), then the church will focus on the proclamation of this message and be a gathering of persons who repent and believe. It is the thesis of this essay that the church must be restructured according to our Christological affirmations. If the crisis-reconciliation motif is able to uncover the power of the gospel for our time, then we will need to construct a view of the church on it, rather than other atonement theories. To the elements of this motif we now turn.

The Divine Initiative

Like all major interpretations of Christ's death and resurrection, the crisis-reconciliation motif originates with a divine initiative. The origin of our salvation lies in God. On this point theories of atonement agree. Where they differ is in their focus on a dominant relationship: God and humanity; God and Satan or death; or internal relations within God. At least three major theories focus on the relation of God and humanity. First, we see this in the legal theories, where Christ satisfies the demands of the law and/or substitutes himself in our place to bear the penalty of the law. Second, it also appears in theories drawing on the Gospel of John and Athanasius, where salvation is the incorporation of humanity into the divine life. Third, Abelard remains within the framework of God's relation to humanity, but shifts the emphasis to the divine love that inspires and evokes a response of love and trust. The focus changes when one considers salvation as liberation from Satanic power, as is the case with Irenaeus. Some might prefer to place Athanasius with Irenaeus, where God's victory over Satan and death is central. In Anselm, where the motif is not legal but commercial, the relation shifts again, this time to internal relations within God (i.e., God's honor). Here the creation has been corrupted by sin, thereby upsetting the divine purpose and placing humankind in debt to God. The incarnation is necessitated because God must be faithful to the divine intention for the world, but only God can restore such an intention. Obviously the playing out of this necessity within God will affect humankind, but it is secondary to God's fidelity to the divine purpose.

In the crisis/reconciliation motif, the focus is on God's relation to humankind, but the issue is more complicated than the violation of the law. Claims to wisdom and power change our relation to God and the world about us. With respect to God, they deny the sovereignty of God, the only true source of wisdom and life-giving power, thereby raising the issue of idolatry. With respect to the world, they create the illusion that human beings are self-made and self-determining. They inevitably result in division and war. As we have noted, boasting is both a theological and a psychological problem for Paul because it defines a person in isolation from God and one's neighbors. For reconciliation to occur, there must be a shattering of such idolatrous claims as well as a redirection of trust from the world to God.

Reconciliation

Every interpretation of Jesus' death and resurrection aims at a particular view of salvation. In the history of Christian thought, the major themes are liberation from demonic powers, the reunion of sinners and a holy/loving God, the restoration of God's intention by the redemption of the world, and the incorporation of humanity into the divine life. In the view developed here, salvation is defined as reconciliation: the uniting of persons with one another and with God according to God's will.

The reconciliation of Jesus Christ is a new basis of union that is inclusive and liberating. It presupposes the removal of the barriers and the competing claims that have divided. To be reconciled means that we are no longer defined by the old divisions, but by a new reality. Therefore reconciliation always involves repentance.

The new reality that binds us together is the grace of God that creates in this world a new place to be. Reconciliation is not pretending that there were no divisions or that nothing has happened. The new basis of union is not our agreement or achievement. It does not depend on our readiness or perfection. Its foundation lies in the will of God that we, who are so divided, be united. This union is not according to the claims of this world, but by God's gracious and life-giving power. Therefore reconciliation always includes hearing the gospel and celebrating the sacraments, which testify to the presence of God.

The reconciliation of Jesus Christ binds us together in the face of our particularity and individuality, inviting us to participate in the household of God. It also binds us together in the face of radical opposition, old wounds, and serious disagreements. Those reconciled are therefore called with Christ to bear the divisions and pain of the world, to overcome evil with good, and to work for the coming Rule of God. Here the witness of a community of faith makes the point. On May 13, 1993, five Amish children were killed by a speeding auto near Fredericksburg, Ohio. The auto was driven by a young man, Eric Bache, who showed no remorse for his action in the days that followed. After the funeral, an elder of the community, Henry Burkholder, said: "We could take it a lot easier if he would feel sorry. It's a little harder to forgive since he doesn't seem upset. But we have to forgive him. And we will."[3] Such a witness to bearing the sin of the world makes it clear that it is not easy. It is a process of living under the rule of Christ and struggling with it; it is bearing the pain and knowing the freedom Christ brings. Those called by Christ are bound to him, and their options are therefore limited to the way of Christ, as difficult as that may appear to the world.

The Centrality of the Cross

In the crisis-reconciliation motif, the crucifixion and resurrection of Jesus are central. They must remain so against the human tendency to remove them from view. There have always

---

3. *New York Times*, May 17, 1993, p. A12. This quote also points up the difference between Anabaptist peace strategy and much of the activism of liberal Protestantism. Whereas the latter tend to see pacifism as a strategy (i.e., love and self-sacrifice are the means to an end, such as winning converts or improving the world), Anabaptists have no illusions about the utilitarian benefits of pacifism. It is mandated by the crucified Lord and is the witness one must make. It is not defended as a means to some end, but as an end in itself. This is not to say, however, that such witness cannot have an influence on others. In 1994 a friend met two visitors to Lancaster County from New York City. When asked what brought them to Lancaster, they replied that they wanted to see the people that could forgive the driver that killed five children in Ohio.

been those offended by a religion that remains tied to an ancient world and that refuses to translate a seemingly arbitrary event into a rational concept. Others take offense at the suggestion that human redemption involves the shedding of innocent blood. Paul anticipates these objections and reminds us to stand firm in keeping the cross and resurrection at the heart of the gospel. To remove the cross from the central message, in an attempt to smooth it out or make it more compatible with our times, is to lose the power of the gospel: "For Christ did not send me to baptize but to preach the gospel, and not with eloquent wisdom, lest the cross of Christ be emptied of its power" (1 Cor. 1:17). There can be no getting around the cross, no going beyond it or rising above it to a higher or purer understanding. It cannot be translated into a concept, cleansed of the unsightly sorrow of Golgotha. The sixteenth-century artist Grünewald was correct in portraying John the Baptist as a witness, with outstretched arm and enlarged finger, pointing to Jesus crucified.

But having affirmed the centrality of cross and resurrection, the question still remains how such events change the world. This is a question about both the reality of the gospel and the language we use to describe it. Since we cannot speak of the reality of the gospel without language, the two sides of the question collapse into one. It is a serious question because we live in a world where, for most people, the old religious worldview has collapsed. Even devoutly religious people are not religious like Christians in the second or sixteenth century. For example, if most of the overarching religious concepts are not part of our worldview, then the interpretation of Jesus' death cannot be by means of a deductive logic, referring to how things *must* take place, or appealing to seldom-used verses of the Old Testament. Such arguments hang by a *necessity* that is itself dependent on a host of assumptions that most people today do not know or accept. Appeals to such a necessity, so common in theories of penal substitution or Anselm's argument for the incarnation, simply lose their force. Or consider the difference between Luther's religious experience and that of people today: if few people awaken each day with Luther's overriding sense of sinfulness in the presence of a righteous God, it will be difficult to explain Jesus' death in terms of the expiation of our sin. Underneath all of these shifts in conceptual framework and experience is the absence of knowledge of the biblical stories: if no one knows the significance of animal sacrifice in ancient Israel, let alone the story of Abraham and Isaac, how can Jesus' life be understood by referring to him as the Lamb of God?[4] Even the modern liberal religious assumption that people are concerned about doing the good needs to be questioned in a culture where the dominant values are individual freedom and personal happiness. In the face of such preoccupation with ourselves, what purpose is there in portraying Jesus as the one who calls us to do the good? In all these cases we see that the challenge facing those who would proclaim the gospel is to speak of the cross in words accessible to our times.

How then shall we speak of the cross? Our discussion alternates between the language of the New Testament and our own experience. Moreover, it proceeds in stages. One begins by answering certain questions, only to find that the answers pose yet another set of questions. For our purposes this is the progression from the more general to the specific.

Let us begin by speaking in general terms of the cross. Following the argument of 1 Corinthians 1–2, God uses the cross in two ways: to shatter the false claims of the world and to embody true wisdom and power. How can the cross shatter

4. While taking the guided tour of the cathedral in Chartres, France, with Malcolm Miller, a group of some 30 people was asked by Miller, "Who was Jesse?" Not one person could answer the question.

false claims? One must keep in mind that wisdom is supposed to enable us to understand the nature of things and the proper relations between them; power is supposed to create life and nurture community. When those who claim wisdom do not understand the things that make for life, or when those who possess power generate only death and division, then questions inevitably are asked: Are they really wise? Is this not an abuse of power? Such acts are not simply counterproductive, they undercut the claims to authority. When a system of justice imprisons or executes the wrong person, such a system is called into question. National policies that generate only endless division or war are finally perceived as self-destructive. The presence of the innocent who suffer exposes the pretensions and hypocrisy of tyrannical powers. It is from this general viewpoint that it can be said that Jesus on the cross in his weakness becomes a greater threat to the world than in his teachings.

But Jesus simultaneously embodies the alternative to the world's wisdom and power. God uses Jesus to create on earth, as with Israel, the reality of life lived for God and neighbor. In his life and teaching, as in his death, Jesus creates a community constituted on an alternative wisdom and power. It is the Rule of God governed by justice and mercy, life-giving power and grace. The cross is not simply a word of judgment; it is an invitation to life. Its twofold purpose corresponds directly to Jesus' admonition in Mark 1:14: repent and believe in the coming of the Rule of God.

If the cross is the means of reconciliation, we must be more specific and ask how this means relates to Jesus himself. Jesus is not used by God in a utilitarian way, to make a point and then be discarded, as if his person were unrelated to the purpose and message. The means is Jesus himself, and what he does embodies the new reality of reconciliation. What he does expresses who he is; his person is truly embodied in his actions. Therefore, we must not simply refer to the cross as the *means* of reconciliation. Restated, the issue becomes this: how does Jesus in his person reconcile, and what is Jesus' relation to the cross?

Here the tradition comes to our aid. For while it is filled with arguments, concepts, symbols, and appeals that are not common to our cultural mind-set, it does offer a treasury of images that are so simple and basic to human experience that they can assist us in hearing the gospel as good news. Two such images, which constitute a fundamental polarity, are the affirmations that Jesus *participates* in our life and *transcends* our life.[5]

From the beginning the followers of Jesus were drawn to Jesus because he participated (i.e., took part) in their life. He was willing to recognize them, identify with them, and share life with them. No wonder the Gospel of John should begin with the affirmation of divine participation: "And the Word became flesh and dwelt among us." But this most grand declaration of participation rests not on the disciples' prior knowledge of who Jesus was, but on their experience of his participation in their life. Nowhere was this more evident than in his rejection, suffering, and death. Like the disciples, Jesus is caught in the warfare of this world, wherein he must bear its anger and hostility. He is rejected and endures the consequences of the world's boasting. The world's powers are un-

5. Those familiar with the history of theology will note the parallel between *participate/transcend* and the affirmations that Jesus Christ is *with us* and *for us*. As is the case with the categories in the traditional Christological discussion, *participate* and *transcend* are not neatly equated with the human and divine in Jesus. Jesus is with us not simply as the human one, nor for us only as the divine one. Divine participation and human transcendence play an important role in most discussions. For good reason the teachers of the early centuries refused to separate or divide humanity and divinity in Jesus in a simple way.

leashed on him because he threatens its claims. From his decision to set his face to Jerusalem to his prayer in Gethsemane, Jesus accepts and endures the suffering of humanity. Like all the innocent who suffer for righteousness' sake, Jesus bears the pain of the world. And like the righteous he endures it in fidelity to God and the coming Rule of God.

Some will take offense at the suggestion that in his suffering Jesus stands among all of the innocent who suffer. Too often Protestantism has so elevated and magnified the suffering of Jesus that he is isolated from us and, as a consequence, does not appear to participate in our life. Such glorification of Jesus only tends to empty the cross of its power. The power of the cross is found in part in its connection with all innocent who suffer. The history of Israel is filled with archetypes of the cross, wherein men and women are persecuted for righteousness' sake. Indeed, it was this tradition in memory and text that provided a treasury of interpretation for the early Christians. Protestants would also do well to reconsider the development of the veneration of Mary in the Middle Ages. Whereas Protestants have traditionally seen such a move as a diminution of Jesus' place in the life of faith, such a judgment misses a powerful opportunity to understand Jesus and our relation to him. When Mary is depicted as the grieving mother bearing the crucified Jesus in her arms, as in paintings and sculpture on countless altars, we have an expansion of Jesus' participation in our life. Instead of isolating Jesus from his family and disciples, such works of art place his suffering in the context of our suffering. The story is expanded to include the mother of Jesus. Mary is presented as the mother who must hold the body of her beloved son. She is as alone and forsaken as he was on the cross. But it is not only Mary who is included and elevated for honor. Consider the women down through the centuries who have viewed such paintings and sculpture: mothers who have held their children dying from sickness and starvation, or mothers who have held their sons and daughters killed in the violence of this world. Cannot these women readily identify with Mary? They share in a common suffering. One can only wonder if the origin and rise of the veneration of Mary were a correction of a tradition that relies so heavily on the language of Father and Son to speak of God's participation in humanity. In contrast to such a partial view of participation, Mary completes the circle. If Mary in her grief and suffering exposes the wrongs of this world, will not the grief and suffering of other mothers also expose the world's injustice? If Mary, in her fidelity to the crucified, is honored by the risen Christ, will not other mothers be honored by Christ for their fidelity?[6]

But while Jesus is marked by his participation in our life, he also appears as one who *transcends* us and the powers of this world. Mark is probably the best account of the way the followers of Jesus came to apprehend this transcendence. Beginning with a one-sentence introduction, without a birth narrative as in Matthew and Luke or a lengthy prologue as in John, Mark announces the appearance of John the Baptist and Jesus. Jesus is baptized and then declares the fulfillment of time in the coming of God's rule. Most important, there then follows a series of events in which Jesus displays the power to attract followers, cast out demons, teach, reinterpret the Scriptures, and gather a community that breaks with the present social and religious conventions. In the face of all of these acts, the new followers and general audience are attracted to Jesus and amazed by him, but they do not know who he is. Only those possessing unclean spirits appear to know who Jesus is (Mark 1:24; 3:11)!

6. On the exterior of the front of the Rheims Cathedral, over the center door, is the stone sculpture of Jesus placing a crown on Mary's head. Does not this honor offered to Mary by her Son, now risen as Lord, witness to the vindication of the faithful who have suffered the loss of their children?

Mark draws us into the story by prompting us to wonder what these people found attractive in Jesus. To be sure, none of the Gospels gives us extended testimonies from all of these people. The stories contain, however, the elements of transcendence that attract and inspire people in every age. In a world of massive social disorder and political repression through military force, Jesus actualizes mercy and justice for the poor and outcasts. There is liberation from lifelong illness and confinement. Persons enduring the burden of shame receive forgiveness of sins. Old ideas that exclude and repress are set aside by a higher truth. Persons who had settled into the routine of life receive a call (vocation). A circle of friendship and acceptance is formed that sets aside the rebuke and disgrace of current conventions. Eyes are turned from the overwhelming sense of a world dominated by demons to the discovery that the world is the creation of a sovereign God. In these and countless ways, Jesus displays in his words and deeds a transcendence that turns the world upside down. The world as his listeners know it has become quite predictable, full of inequalities and sufferings. It is a world of conflicting forces. What attracts people to Jesus is his ability to envision a new world. As the word *transcend* implies, he *rises above* what has become the routine, predictable, and known world. Perhaps the rougher meaning of *transcend* catches the point even better: Jesus *climbs over* the expected world and points to the reign of God. *Rise above* has connotations of leaving or ignoring the world; *climb over* suggests conflict and struggle, a living in and with the world but not being bound by it.

In his person, which finds expression in acts and relations with those about him, Jesus is the means of reconciliation. He embodies the reign of God that is both present and coming. Nowhere is this more evident than in his fidelity to God in the face of opposition and rejection. Against the ever-present concern for self and the fear of death that govern life, Jesus lives

119

in the presence of God's justice and mercy. It is here, at this central point of his fidelity and witness to God, that Jesus is the means of reconciliation. By this life for God and against the world Jesus actualizes the will of God to reconcile heaven and earth. His willingness to bear the suffering inflicted on him by the powers of the world, and to resist those powers by refusing to respond in kind, is the means of reconciliation. Through such bearing and resistance Jesus breaks the power of the world to govern him. In refusing to answer in kind (i.e., with anger against his opponents and/or God, or with demands for vengeance), he breaks the cycle of violence. Like all who suffer for righteousness' sake, Jesus earned the right to demand vengeance. But he refuses, knowing that such an act will only continue the cycle of blood vengeance. As one who has the right to ask for retaliation, Jesus points to a love that takes into itself the violence of the world without being overcome. In raising Jesus from the dead, for the sake of good news rather than judgment, God reveals a justice and mercy that can aim only at life rather than death.

As the embodiment of such a new reality, it is clear that Jesus redefines transcendence over against the dominant images of worldly wisdom and power. There is an obvious correlation between what scholars have called the secret of Mark's Gospel and Paul's play on the words *wisdom* and *power.* If there is a secret in Mark that is hidden from the view of disciples, onlookers, and opponents (cf. Mark 4), it is that the Rule of God shall come into the world by means of sacrificial love displayed in Jesus' rejection and crucifixion. For Paul, what the world judges to be foolishness and weakness is revealed to be divine wisdom and power. In both cases, transcendence as the symbol of divine presence and/or life-giving power is redefined. It cannot be any other way, since there cannot be reconciliation between God and the world, or between human beings, on the basis of the competing claims of the world.

But if transcendence is redefined by the cross, then our vocabulary about God, as well as our understanding of God, is changed. Jesus does more than shatter the wisdom and power of the world. Every social critic and moral protest does that. The early Christians see in Jesus' cross and resurrection good news because they reveal *God's* wisdom and power. As Paul exclaims: "God was in Christ reconciling the world to himself" (2 Cor. 5:19). Or consider the designation of Jesus as the Lamb of God, who takes away the sin of the world. This is as much a statement about God's willingness to bear the sins of the world as about Jesus' engagement with sin. Jesus is not a Lamb *for* God, but the Lamb *of* God. What Jesus bears, God bears. If there is any doubt, we must simply ask: how are sins taken away? Where can sins be hidden from God? Where can we put them that they will no longer cause anger and division, remind us of former wrongs, or inspire a desire for retaliation? The answer is quite clear: in bearing the sins of the world, God takes them into the divine life and overcomes them. In Jesus of Nazareth it is God who wills to reconcile human beings with one another and with God. God bears within the divine life all of the anger and violence of the world. The circle of blood vengeance is ended because God will not perpetuate it. All of this makes it absolutely understandable and essential for the church of the fourth century to have rejected Arius's contention that the transcendent God could not be in Jesus. Against Arius, the church affirmed that Jesus redefines transcendence. The incarnation is a statement about God and our salvation.

Let us conclude this section by reviewing the distance traveled. We began by affirming the centrality of the crucifixion and resurrection in the crisis-reconciliation motif. We focused on how it is possible for such acts to be the means of reconciliation. This drew us to the conclusion that it is not these acts per se but Jesus himself that is the means of reconciliation, through his fidelity to God and embodiment of new life. But as with all theories of atonement, we have concluded by affirming that cross and resurrection are not simply statements about means, or even Jesus, but ultimately about God. Cross and resurrection are the means of our reconciliation as well as a revealing of the divine life in our presence, inviting us to partake of such life.

The Objectivity/Subjectivity Polarity

In the vocabulary of historical theology, theories of atonement are usually tested by what are called objective and subjective elements. The former refers to something that actually happened that is decisive for salvation. The latter refers to how the saving event becomes effective in the believer, especially across time and space. Some theories are obviously stronger on one element than the other, though in the end they must include both. While legal substitution theories dramatically declare that "Christ died for our sins," such an objective event still leaves open the question of how that death is appropriated for one's salvation. Conversely, the theory associated with Abelard has usually been criticized for its overemphasis on the love of God that inspires faith in the believer. But even this criticism can be overdone, since all of the theories must in the end deal with Abelard's point: human beings must be inspired to love God through the disclosure of the grace in Jesus Christ, whether we are speaking of liberation from Satan or release from the penalty of the law.

The crisis-reconciliation motif affirms both sides of the objective/subjective polarity. Reconciliation is the shattering of the false claims of the world and the actualization of the new reality in Jesus Christ. In his resurrection as Lord, Jesus is a sign of the new humanity and the new age. The continuation of his covenant community, now commissioned to proclaim the gospel of reconciliation, is irrevocable. If the Gospels take Jesus' reading of Isaiah 61 as verification of the presence of the Rule of God, Paul can point to the church as the uniting of all things in Christ: Jew and Gentile, male and female, slave and free, rich and poor. The world has been changed and shall be changed.

One way of testing the objectivity of a theory is by means of the old question, was Jesus' death really necessary? In some popular versions of transactional theories, where Jesus pays the penalty for guilty sinners, his death is both absolutely necessary and the efficient cause of salvation. The world would not be redeemed if Jesus had not died. As one can imagine, such logic inevitably prompts the reaction that it makes Jesus' death the propitiation of an angry God. In the name of love and mercy, such a view is denounced, very often in ways that suggest Jesus' death is incidental to the process. How then does our theory answer the question?

The crisis-reconciliation motif bases the certainty or as-surance of salvation in God and what God does, not in some-thing done to God. It is God who anoints Jesus with the Spirit, sustains him in his suffering, and raises him from the dead as Lord. If there is a decisive moment of reconciliation, it is in Jesus' fidelity to God and his resistance to the powers of the world. Reconciliation is actualized in the world in God's willing-ness to bear (i.e., take into the divine life) the violence of the cross and not retaliate with violence, but create a community of life. Jesus' death is a consequence of this saving power. Given the conflicting claims and powers of the world, it is predictable and inevitable. It rightly symbolizes the fidelity of Jesus and the love of God.

What then of the subjective side in this theory of recon-ciliation? To speak strongly of God's action in Jesus Christ does not negate a human response. Indeed, it aims at the incor-poration of humanity into the new community marked by faith, hope, and love. Paul declares in his second letter to the Corinthians that he is an ambassador for Christ: God is making an appeal to them through him (2 Cor. 5:20). The reconciliation that is a reality in Jesus Christ must be actualized in the Corinthians. While this process is not one of human achievement (works) in accordance to moral demands, it does require a response from them. They cannot receive the gifts of the new creation, where members are not regarded from a human point of view (2 Cor. 5:16), unless they are willing to set aside the wisdom and power of the world. This is accomplished only by incorporation into the new reality by a trust of the heart, wherein the believer relinquishes control of identity and worth based on worldly standards and receives identity and worth as gifts of God. In the Corinthian letters such a change is envisioned as being out of one's mind, when viewed according to the world's standards (2 Cor. 5:13). In Philippians it is having a new mind (Phil. 2:5). In Romans 6 it is described as the transition from an old selfhood to a new selfhood in the new life of Jesus Christ, a change of such magnitude that Paul compares it to a death and resurrection of the believer. That such a transition is linked with baptism joins the response of the believer with the initiating and transforming grace of God. Human action and change are required, but they are always a response to and in the context of the empowering and nurturing grace that surrounds and upholds us. We are willing and able to give up the old selfhood only because we are drawn by a grace to see a new possibility in Jesus Christ. But while our faith, hope, and love are the necessary embrace of the gracious God, our response is never the basis for that grace. No matter what happens in our response, be it great or small, whether it vacillates between hot, cold, and lukewarm, the certainty of our reconciliation always rests in a divine will that envisions all things united in Christ.

A New Reality

Just as the crisis-reconciliation motif holds in tension the objective/subjective polarity, it also sets forth the double affirmation: salvation is a new reality, which is both present and future. It is clear that Paul understands this dialectic and lives in it. It cannot be emphasized enough for our time. Paul is painfully aware that he and the Corinthians have not completely actualized the new reality. The powers of this world, the alienation within and among them, and the desire to claim too much for themselves continue to be present in their lives and the world. Nevertheless the reunion of God and humankind, as well as the reconciliation of divided humanity, is a new reality. Paul speaks in the past and present tenses in describing what God *has done* in Jesus Christ and *is doing* now. This is a possibility because the reality of reconciliation rests in God and not ourselves. The gospel is not a proposal or strategy given to us, as if we could or must actualize it by ourselves in some future time. The gospel is not an offer contingent on our compliance by means of moral and political correctness. It is not a gift dependent on our readiness for improvement. If any of these demands were requirements for the entrance of salvation into the world, then it would never be present. Paul experiences and proclaims reconciliation as a new reality in the present because of what God has done in the cross and resurrection of Jesus. It is God who "is the source of your life in Christ Jesus, whom God made our wisdom, our righteousness and sanctification and redemption; therefore, as it is written, 'Let him who boasts, boast of the Lord'" (1 Cor. 1:30-31).

It is precisely because reconciliation is a present reality that Paul can admonish the Corinthians, as well as all recipients of his letters, to actualize this new reality in their lives. Of course Paul sees the sin and division still present in his life and the lives of his brothers and sisters. But in his view, there is little point in practical admonitions unless there has been a substantive change in our situation, which will enable new life. Though he never mentions Jesus' reference to the good tree that bears good fruit, Paul's general theory of the Christian life rests squarely on such an idea. Doing proceeds from being. Paul's admonitions are fundamentally a call to become what we are already in Christ. There is the possibility of change and growth because Christ, as the new reality, is already in us and the world. "Now we have received not the spirit of the world, but the Spirit which is from God, that we might understand the gifts bestowed on us by God" (1 Cor. 2:12).

Liberation

The crisis-reconciliation motif also makes clear that we cannot divide reconciliation from liberation. To separate them is to destroy them. There can be no reconciliation unless we are liberated from the bondage to the claims of this world, which at the deepest level insist that we are the source of our salvation. But liberation from falsehood and the powers of this world will not be complete unless we stand in that new place with both God and our neighbor. What we have seen in our analysis of 1 Corinthians 1–2 is that, instead of being divided, both reconciliation and liberation are present. Human beings are in bondage to a false wisdom and power, which perpetuate the hostility and divisions of the world. There is a false consciousness as well as trust in false gods. From this perspective, reconciliation cannot occur if human beings will not relinquish their ultimate claims to wisdom and power. The liberation from these ultimate claims by means of the power of the cross opens the possibility of a new relation with human beings and with God.

If we add 2 Corinthians 5 to the picture, we can see that reconciliation and liberation are always held together, but even more important, reconciliation is the final goal of salvation. It is not enough to shatter the idols; salvation represents the reality of new life. Freedom is always the freedom to be in Christ and with one another. Life with one another is not something added on to liberated persons; life together is the purpose of our liberation. The church is by definition a community of persons, open and inclusive, because its very existence is bound to the reconciling work of God in Jesus Christ.

The Gospel of Reconciliation: A Theology for Opposites, Differences, and Enemies

We are now at a point where we can begin the transition to the rebuilding of our theology of the church. From the start, this essay has argued that thinking about the church must be based on our most fundamental affirmations regarding the gospel of Jesus Christ. We also noted earlier in this chapter that most views of the church are directly linked to views of Jesus Christ. For both reasons this chapter began with a discussion of the cross. This led us to an interpretation where crisis and reconciliation join together as the central motif: the gospel is a crisis because false claims are unveiled for what they are; it is reconciliation because God has created a new basis of union. But to move from an interpretation of the meaning of Jesus Christ to the church still requires an intermediate step. We need to draw out of this primary analysis the guidelines or norms that will govern our understanding of the proclamation of the gospel as well as the rebuilding of the church. Such norms must be clearly *drawn out of,* rather than *pushed into,* the Christological affirmations that describe the root experience of faith. They must also signal the direction both proclamation and ecclesiology must take for us in our time.

127

Living without Ultimate Claims, Save One

If Paul could find a connection between claims to power and wisdom in Corinth and the crucifixion of Jesus, he would not have much trouble finding such a connection in modern America. From cradle to grave we are defined by claims about ourselves, which confer grace or disgrace. Added to the traditional ways our achievements define us are the defining marks of our times: the quest for independence or differentiation, victimization, anger, and ideological warfare. Against all of these attempts to define our identity and worth by worldly standards, the gospel is an end to all ultimate claims, save one. To receive the gospel is to acknowledge that the cross is a word of judgment against our confidence in the conventional wisdom and the current balance of powers. To hear the word of grace given to you is to discover that your identity and worth are gifts of God. It is also to enter into a new world where one can live without claiming wisdom and power, because the world's wisdom and powers no longer control us. It is as Jesus predicts: "For those who want to save their life will lose it, and those who lose their life for my sake, and for the sake of the gospel, will save it" (Mark 8:35 NRSV). The gospel is an end to the life of claiming, except for the one claim that God is gracious and wills life. To receive the Rule of God is to be defined once and for all by God.

If this gospel means freedom from the terror of one's own self-doubt and inner demons, it also means freedom from the claims of our ideological warfare. The cross reveals that something is wrong with the cultural ideology of American religion. Instead of producing the promised justice, equality, and happiness, it produces exclusion and division, suffering and warfare. This judgment is directed to both the left-wing and right-wing versions of our cultural ideology. Both versions rest fundamentally on the same claims: that we are innocent, that we give ourselves identity and worth by what we do, and that the solution to social conflict is to impose our view on the other side. But the latter is impossible. On the one side, the left wing embraces the culture of individualism and self-actualization. So open to the relativism of the culture, it is in danger of sacrificing the heritage. The priority of individual liberty usually entails the subordination of ethical norms. The Bible is used for justification, but too often as an afterthought, without a clear affirmation that Scripture has an authority in and of itself. By contrast, the right wing retreats into the protective world of biblical and doctrinal fundamentalism, where legalism replaces the grace of the gospel. In an attempt to protect the gospel from the modern world, the right wing claims the absolute authority of every verse of the Bible, a claim that is impossible to defend. Such a claim is also denied by the radical selectivity of the special social agenda of the right wing. In practice, the conservatives do not value every verse, but only those verses that support their vision of the world. Having moved to opposite extremes, neither left nor right can understand the other, nor point to common ground. Each only arouses in the other basic fears: the left fears tyrannical repression and the right fears chaos and anarchy. Each sees what it fears in the other. While they cannot save each other, they can wound each other and perpetuate the cultural war.

In his essay on the contemporary church, Leander Keck illuminates the way innocence is central to the way Americans define themselves.

> When Yale's R. W. B. Lewis coined the phrase "the American adam," he saw the point, though he is not responsible for my reading of Adam. The American Adam is both innocent and perfectible because he did not experience the "Fall" and so has no significant complicity in the evils that beset him; rather he is an innocent victim who, if but liberated from the evil structures imposed by society, and from the malign influence of neurotic parents, will flourish and perfect him-

self by actualizing all his possibilities. So long as his acts do not infringe too much on another person's rights, anything is permitted that fulfills him. This Adam can be a loner or a joiner, for he is an autonomous person, whose social relationships are a matter of contract — arrangements that can be made, changed, unmade, as needed or desired. For the American Adam, the word "God" is a symbol for the power that is available for pursuing one's goals. His offspring are not Cain and Abel, or Moses viewing Canaan from afar, but Ralph Waldo Emerson and Horatio Alger. . . . This Adam is now burdened by enormous guilt, on the one hand, for succeeding in the past by nearly exterminating Native Americans along with native bison, and, on the other hand, for not succeeding in the present. We condemn ourselves as failures if our bodies are not slim, if we are not perfect parents, if our children are not achievers too, if we do not get promoted continually. In short, if you have problems with your life, it's probably your fault. And while there is truth in that, it is haunted by illusions.

This is an extremely rich analysis of our cultural ideology, partly because it links the major elements of American consciousness: innocence, perfectibility, self-reliance, individualism, action, and guilt. It is also rich because it can be applied to both sides in the culture war. Consider the way innocence is fundamental to both liberal and conservative ideology. In the liberal version, there is a basic optimism regarding the individual. If evil exists, it takes form in repressive social forces. In the conservative version, evil is definitely real, but lodged in specific acts of behavior by individuals against the social order; it is not present in cultural forces that extend over time nor in the broad patterns of ideas or behavior in social institutions. On either side the individual is still free from the more radical view of sin found in the Bible. The one side denies the presence of excessive self-love, self-deception, or ill will, affirming the innate goodness of the individual; the other side denies any complicity with institutionalized ill will (e.g., racism or robber-baron capitalism) since they did not commit these acts in the previous century and there is no admission that present structures embody such tendencies.

In both sides this claim to innocence leads to confidence in the perfectibility of the individual as well as his/her program. If liberals are prone to point up the evils of the social order or the previous generation (i.e., their parents), they are confident that they will be free from them. Conversely, conservatives play down criticism of the current social order and the tradition in the confidence that it is the best we can achieve, if not in fact perfect. Both assume that we make ourselves by our action and that we are perfectible. Both suggest in direct or subtle ways that everything depends on what we do: either we must create a new social order free from the evils of the past or we must reaffirm and maintain traditional values against the forces of chaos. On these terms everything depends on human action, be it the improvement of society, one's personal success, or one's salvation. One is saved by one's moral action or the strength of one's faith. Given the centrality of human agency, God is viewed from a utilitarian perspective, stripped of sovereignty to act according to a divine plan, but ready to assist and sanctify each rival program.

If there is any doubt about how each version of the culture war rests on a claim to innocence (i.e., perfect wisdom and power), consider the willingness of each side to establish a test for membership in the church. The social, moral, and political agenda of each side becomes the basis for union. Such a willingness to sort out the sheep from the goats can happen only if one believes one is absolutely right. It is at this point that the legalism and self-righteousness of each side emerges. Either one must agree with the particular version or one is condemned. In a parallel manner, each side has no compunctions about the use of power. On the left, power is the key concept for analysis and strategy; on the right, power is divinely given to limit and/or strike down unbelievers (cf. the rhetoric of the anti-abortion activists).

If both rely so heavily on a claim to innocence, how does guilt fit into this picture? In theory it is something to be avoided, because it would deny innocence. If we had to admit that our hearts are prone to self-deception and ill will, capable of inordinate selfishness, the left-wing ideology would crumble. Likewise, if we had to admit that we live in a social/historical environment, which includes traditions of repression and inequality that have both benefited us and oppress us, the right-wing ideology would crumble. In spite of their denials, both sides inevitably encounter guilt because they live in a world where everything depends on the individual. When they must face the fact that they have failed, they are confronted by guilt. Since they have no experience of what is involved in Luther's confession that we live simultaneously with a sense of sin and grace, this crisis is unbearable. But if one cannot live with guilt, it must be avoided. This avoidance takes different forms: on the left guilt can be avoided by directing anger at the repressive forces or by doing something to solve the problem; on the right, guilt can be avoided by denial and conspiracy theories directed against criticism (e.g., compare the claims that the Holocaust never occurred, or that slavery in American was a humane institution).

We are living at a time when the cultural ideology present in the church and society is both obsolete and destructive. Neither version can liberate because it does not know the radical repentance required of the gospel, wherein we are forced to admit that the problem is in us. Neither version can reconcile because it cannot point to a place where all people can stand. Instead each insists the other side accept unconditional surrender. In such a situation there is little hope, unless the Word of the cross is spoken to both sides.

The Peace of Christ in a Violent World

The gospel of reconciliation points to a new reality in our midst. This reality is a new way of being in the world. It is a gathering of people who are *opposite* (e.g., male and female), *different* (i.e., by virtue of race, class, and personal interest), and *enemies* into a place where they can exist together. This place is the peace of Christ. It is a sanctuary that belongs to God, because only God in Christ can create a place where partisan claims do not count. This place is a peaceful place because here we find a basis of union not constructed on human agreement or domination by one side. We are constrained by the crucified Christ to set aside our preference for war; we are drawn into this place by a vision of life rather than death.

A powerful example of how God creates a new place, against every expectation, is seen in the agreement of mutual recognition between the Palestinian Liberation Organization and Israel in September 1993. Both sides chose to begin a process away from the cycle of death. But for so many people on both sides, this meant doing the unthinkable: recognizing the enemy. In defense of his signing of such an agreement, the Israeli prime minister, Yitzhak Rabin, stated, "Peace is not made with friends. Peace is made with enemies, some of whom — and I won't mention names — I loathe very much."[7]

These words are so powerful precisely because they are so obvious. They catch the imagination because they clear away the sentimental and naive notions of making peace: it is not worked out with those we like; it is not easy; it is not imposing our will on the other. Peace begins only when opposing sides are willing and able to adopt a new beginning. It requires a new basis of union, in which both sides will begin to engage in work — hard work, even harder than war itself — directed

7. *New York Times*, September 5, 1993, sec. 4, p. 1.

toward living together in the face of old divisions and differences.

From a human perspective such a way of being in the world is unthinkable. In our world of bitter conflict, fostered and perpetuated by ancient prejudices and new acts of violence, it is unthinkable to be with those who either are not like us or are our enemies. But from the view of the cross it is thinkable because it is grounded in God. It is there for us to see, trust, and celebrate because it is not founded on human agreement. It is from first to last the work of the reconciling God, who bears the hostility of the world and wills to overcome it. It is in our midst because God will not treat us the way we wish to treat one another. If God had done so, there would never have been the mark of Cain, the sign of Noah, the promise to Abraham and Sarah, the call of Moses, or the baptism of Jesus. The new reality, which we call the peace of Christ, is always a gift. It is given by God in love for the healing of our hearts and minds, for the reconciliation of all peoples.

But even unthinkable gifts must be received. Sometimes they are taken, but not received or accepted. They are often set aside and ignored. In some cases they are resisted. The peace of Christ is not a magical transformation of everything or everyone. It is definitely not something imposed on people by force. It is the new basis of union, present now right in our midst, offering life rather than death. At a most fundamental level one can say that the alternative to the mutual recognition of opposites, differences, and enemies is Bosnia: a nightmare of terror and destruction. Yet though we see that as a possible future for the entire world, the gospel does not intimidate or threaten us. It is not a new form of spiritual violence. Contrary to the practice of fire-and-brimstone preaching, the gospel draws us into the place of Christ by offering to us a new future. We who once defined ourselves according to the wisdom and powers of the world, who are so separated from God and one another, are declared to be sons and daughters of God and brothers and sisters in Christ. In the peace of Christ there is the possibility of defining ourselves according to what God sees in us and does for and with us. This is an alternative to our self-definitions based on anger and even our suffering. It is to be drawn into a place where violence is put to an end by the God who bears in the divine life the violence of the world. It is this God who declares peace, who makes peace with us, and invites us to be in a place of peace.

The Peace of Christ:
Starting Out from Where We Want to Be

The peace of Christ is in our midst as the new reality, and it is our future. The reconciling work of God must be understood eschatologically, holding together the presence of God's Rule and our prayers for its final manifestation. As a present reality it already contains the future. It is a place in which, and from which, all parties can begin to live and work toward understanding each other in terms of the peace of Christ. In this sense the peace of Christ makes imperative the resistance to the warfare of the world. Those in the peace of Christ are commanded to be reconciled and to be agents of reconciliation; but such action is itself made possible by the presence of the peace of Christ. In this sense we are to become what God has already accomplished.

In the third chapter of the Letter of James there is an imaginative twist on the normal usage of language, conveying the sense of this eschatological reality. "And a harvest of righteousness is sown in peace for those who make peace" (James 3:18). Using the analogy of seedtime and harvest, the verse suggests a causal order between activities. Certain actions will produce certain results. Normally we think of peace as the result of certain activities, including moral virtues. This makes peace dependent on establishing the right conditions for peace. We even have a prophetic warning against declaring peace when there is no peace. As a result, this approach places peace in the future, making it a reality absent from the present. By contrast, James declares that peace is not the result but the cause, not the end but the beginning. Peace is not caused by righteousness or by other moral virtues, such as love or mercy. Rather, righteousness results from sowing peace. Can such a reversal of thinking occur except on the basis of an eschatological understanding of the peace of Christ? The peace of Christ is not a future event, waiting for either God or humans to actualize it by getting all the conditions in place. It is now, and its present reality makes possible new realities. In effect, one must start out from where one wants to be. It is the new reality that defines us and gives us the imperative to become what God would have us be: reconciled.

It is in the context of this eschatological reality that certain major issues of the Christian life must be placed for reflection and action. First, in the peace of Christ those claimed by the new basis of union are joined together in community. It is a violation of the peace of Christ to suggest that a person or a group can be in the peace of Christ and not be bound by Christ with all those in Christ. Christian community must therefore be defined and explored in light of the reconciling work of God.

Second, to be in the peace of Christ is to participate in the common life of believers and the world, as Christ himself participated in our life. Participation means that we are recognized and acknowledged in our particularity and that we recognize and acknowledge our neighbor, who has special gifts and needs. As we observed in the PLO-Israeli agreement, it begins with mutual recognition. If mutual recognition sounds like too little a thing for the Christian life, we need only ask what would happen if we granted mutual recognition to one another? If husbands and wives would grant mutual recognition to one another? Or parents and children? What if whites and blacks granted to each other mutual recognition, or if the nations of wealth recognized the poor of the world? Such mutual recognition would require participation in the life of one another.

Third, to be in the peace of Christ means witness against the claims and warfare of the world. It places one in resistance to them, because those in the peace of Christ refuse to be controlled by the repressive and destructive powers of the world. But the key to such resistance is not returning anger and violence against the world's anger and violence. It is the witness to the way of Christ: returning good for evil. Such resistance represents in our lives the presence of Christ, who bears the violence of the world and returns good for evil. The peace of Christ does have a radical activism, but not like the world's strategies, based on claims to righteousness and employing threats of violence. The peace of the world must be sown in peace.

Fourth and last, to emphasize what hopefully is already obvious, the peace of Christ is a spiritual reality, proclaimed and nurtured by the sacraments. It is ironic that the good news of reconciliation has always been right before us in the liturgy of the Lord's Supper. Perhaps this is a judgment against our hardness of heart or our infatuation with the wisdom and power of the world. The gospel of reconciliation is always present in the celebration of the peace of Christ, now in the face of all conflict and division, yet creating a new basis of union. Perhaps the reform of the church should begin just there, with the peace of Christ given in bread and wine. There in the true treasure of the church is the vision of what God would have us be, calling us to forsake the strategies of domination and grow into the mind of Christ.

CHAPTER 5

The Church as an Image
of Reconciliation

The thesis of this essay is that the doctrine of the church must be rebuilt on the reconciliation revealed in Jesus Christ. The general argument for a theological reform of the church has now become more specific. It is not just any theology or theory of atonement to which we appeal, but a quite specific one. We do this not because the interpretation of the cross in Chapter Four is the only valid one. Indeed, the other theories continue to point to essential aspects of the salvation revealed in Jesus Christ. Rather, the case for rebuilding the church on this interpretation of the cross rests entirely on the overwhelming awareness that we live in a divided world, where alienation and warfare are the dominant characteristics. We are not arguing that this approach to atonement and church is the only valid one, but that it is more appropriate.

The church must recover its priceless treasure, which for our time is the proclamation of reconciliation. In the presence of that gift and promise, the church must be reconstituted. Only such a reformulation of ecclesiology can be faithful to the gospel or be good news to a divided world. The challenge Christians face today is whether they can affirm a basis of unity for themselves as well as for the world. This means that the church must be liberated from the cultural captivity of American religion: the limitations imposed by individualism and functionalism; the loss of transcendence when defined by social/political language as a voluntary association; its complicity in the current ideological warfare of society. To the extent that the church is also divided by competing views of its nature and mission, the church itself contributes to its own fragmentation. Against these forces that have robbed the church of its authority and reduced it to another social organization competing for power, the church must reclaim a language derived from the gospel.

This thesis assumes that there is a strong correlation between a view of Christ and a view of the church. Christian history makes this evident. Theories of atonement that focus on the problem of sin as a barrier between God and humanity are directly tied to the church as a sacramental system conveying the means of grace. When such a system becomes repressive with respect to both the gospel and the life of Christians, as it did in the sixteenth century, a reform occurs. Luther appeals to an alternate reading of the gospel, which also produces an alternate view of the church. The ecclesiology emerging from Luther was dominated by the proclamation of the Word of grace and the new liberty of all Christians to manifest their baptismal calling in service to God and neighbor. Centuries later in America, a highly individualistic religion emerges, where the dominant theories of atonement focus on the sin of individuals and explain how Christ dies for *you*. On such terms, the church is an association of believers, understood functionally as the means whereby God calls individuals to personal salvation. Horrified at the implications of such a view, liberal Protestantism affirms Jesus as the witness to God's Rule in the social realm, calling Christians to service. The mission of the church has been altered by a different Christology, but the church is still understood functionally as a means to an end.

It is not necessary to argue for a simple causal relation between Christology and ecclesiology. It would be far too simplistic to argue that believers always first arrived at a highly developed view of Christ and then organized the church. The church was first constituted by the confession of the Lordship of Jesus, the remembrance of a core of teachings, and the Lord's Supper. But the New Testament also makes it quite clear that problems in organizing the church forced them to reconsider just who Jesus was and is. Christ as the author of a new covenant that sets aside the law is significant in the context of a Jewish/Gentile church. Christ the Lord over the principalities and powers of this world is significant in the face of the claims of the Roman Empire. Paul could hardly have developed the argument of 1 Corinthians 1–2 except in response to the Corinthian conflict. The point is not whether the view of Christ or the view of the church comes first, but that they correlate with one another. A particular view of Christ will inspire a particular constitution of the church, just as a view of the church finds its authority in images of Christ found in the tradition about him.

This reform of the church, which we have repeatedly called a theological reform, must not be misread in either of the following ways. First, it should not be understood as a reactionary counterrevolution in the face of modern culture, based on exclusive forms of church life and/or a narrow doctrinal confessionalism. A reform that is in fact a return to times past will of necessity evoke a mixed response. Among those concerned about an inclusive and liberating church, it will evoke anxiety. Their fear of reimposing all of the old oppressive systems will block any consideration. Among those who believe that reform will occur if we only reinstitute the classic creeds and confessions (or the infallibility of the Bible, and perhaps the social organization connected with times past), it will evoke interest. Against both the anxiety of some and the interest of others, this theological reform takes as its standard the gospel of reconciliation. Such a standard, as we have demonstrated, will not be confined by the theory or practice of either the left or the right, by modern culture or religious dogmatism. If modern culture can stand by in the face of Bosnia, then it demonstrates beyond any doubt that it has neither the wisdom nor the power to reconcile. For different reasons, a strictly dogmatic approach will not unite us. The pluralism of Christianity in America means that we do not share the same confessional documents. The theological reform advocated here assumes that it cannot take its signal from culture, nor go back in time to a golden age of confession. Rather, it must look to the present, when God in Christ is resisting the powers of evil and reconciling the world.

Second, it must not be understood as opposed to an analysis of the church from other perspectives. The church defined theologically is still a community in this world. As such it can and must be examined from various perspectives: social, political, organizational, financial, aesthetic, and so on. Anyone wishing to participate in leadership in the church needs to be conversant with such analysis. What this essay opposes is the willingness to define the church only from these perspectives, so as to neglect or deny the true essence of the church found in the gospel itself.

God's Gift: The Priority of Being

What language shall we use to define the church? Given the way we have come, through an examination of the life of the church and its own theological pluralism, such a question must be taken seriously. We choose to construct this definition of the church by means of the language of being and doing. *Being* refers to the essence of a thing; *doing* refers to the way it exists as a living reality in the world. If the former implies defining marks that give it particular character and a continuing presence, the latter implies the complete range of activities and expressions, internal and external relations, that are necessary for its existence. The language of being and doing allows us to focus on what constitutes the essence of the church. From the beginning, this essay has been primarily about the church's being, and the relation of being and doing. The challenge, however, is to make a distinction between the two without dividing them. In reality they are not separable. There is no churchly being that does not manifest certain practices. The being and doing of the church, as we shall argue, are not two parts of the church's life. They are not to be identified with two places, offices, seasons, or agendas. They are not two tasks, with members given the option of signing up for one or the other. The oneness of the church is not to be divided by the use of this distinction. We are dealing with a logical distinction that enables us to focus on the origin and nature of the church, in contrast to its expressions of faith and order, daily life and practice.

But why then make the distinction? On the one hand it is inevitable that we ask of the essence of the church, its abiding presence, its origin, and the source on which everything rests. Such questions point in a different direction than questions about our life and work together or in the world. On the other hand, the answer lies in the fact that so much of the disorder of American Protestantism arises when there is no clarity about the church's being or doing. Such a situation makes the church vulnerable to the loss of its identity and produces endless disputes about praxis. It also allows both the left and the right to substitute doing for being, thereby turning the gospel into a new form of legalism and moralism. Unless we can at some point distinguish being and doing, the church is always in danger of being defined by its doing.

Let us begin then, in the face of our American preference for action and practice, to speak of the being of the church. We propose that the reform of the church can take place only if we recover the affirmation that the church is a divinely created community. It is the union of God and the world. This new reality is created by God in the crucifixion and resurrection of Jesus Christ. This reconciliation is the basis for our union, in contrast to every worldly claim based on power, wisdom, or human characteristic. The church, as a new reality and basis of union, is not something we create, work toward, or enhance. There can be no conditions for receiving or achieving entrance, except repentance and faith. From first to last it is God's gift. It is the Word made flesh against all of the competing ideological words of this age. To confess one, holy, catholic church is to point to the embodiment of reconciliation as a gift of God in this world.

This is not the way we normally speak of the church. In fact, it goes against our assumptions about the church in very fundamental ways. On the one hand, it is opposed to our preoccupation with subjectivity: that is, our assumption that nothing is real unless we believe it, or that nothing will happen unless we do it. This definition of the church assumes that God is real, is present in the world, and is actually doing something whether we like it or not. Our discomfort with this definition reveals our refusal to let God be God and to look with wonder at the presence of the resurrection in our midst. On the other hand, this definition flies in the face of our moral passion. We have assumed that reconciliation is the absence of alienation and the resolution of conflict. We are willing to be reconciled to those near and far, family members and enemies, when they have changed their evil ways. Since we believe that we are the ones offended, reconciliation cannot occur until they stop doing what we consider offensive.

Thus we hear the words: "I can't be reconciled unless. . . ." From the standpoint of moral passion, there are grounds for such righteous indignation and such preconditions. But is this not also the basis for the moralism and legalism that perpetuate the alienation and conflict? Does this not assume that we are in the right and that we will set the conditions for reconciliation with other people? Even worse, it assumes that the world must be redeemed before a word of grace shall be spoken. If God were to take this stance, would there have been a call to Abraham and Sarah, a burning bush that caused Moses to stop, or an announcement to Mary? God is the only one who has the right to set such conditions for reconciliation. The presence of Israel and of Jesus Christ means that God has chosen not to condemn us, but to reconcile us.

But still the objection comes: "How can you speak of the church as the reality of reconciliation when Christians fight as violently against one another as non-Christians? Even among friendly folks in a local congregation, is there not a long way to go before they fully embody the unity of Christ?" It would be easy, and quite appropriate, to respond from a tactical perspective. Since American religion has moved to the extreme of the priority of doing, what we now need to do is reverse this with an overstatement regarding being. But neither theology nor the life of the church is served well by overstatements and extremes, which divide what is one. We must affirm the reality of God's gift of reconciliation in the here and now, even the weakness and brokenness of the church, because it is there as the foundation on which everything rests. At the heart of the gospel is the declaration that the power of salvation is fully present in the peace of Christ for us to receive, celebrate, and rely on. That peace is a basis of union now; it is also a process that allows us to become what God has already declared in Christ, that is, that we are one. By contrast, the cultural religion of both left and right posits the individual as self-creating and the determiner of the future. This self creates the church and works toward its full actualization, defined on its terms. Everything is controlled and determined by the power and authority of the individual. Such a belief system has failed us, leaving us at war with ourselves. It is also contrary to the eschatological proclamation of the New Testament, which declares that we live in between the coming of the Rule of God and its final consummation.

From this perspective the church and its essential forms must be redefined in terms of the new being of reconciliation:

1. The church is the union of persons with God in Christ, created by God to demonstrate, represent, and celebrate the new life God gives to the world.

2. The church does not have parts, but is present in the world in multiple forms: as a congregation is a union of believers in a particular place, so regional, national, and worldwide gatherings are unions of individuals and congregations created to demonstrate, represent, and celebrate the unity Christ brings to the world. In a similar extension of the mandate to be agents of reconciliation, institutions created for the purposes of education, healing, care, service, and witness are equally forms of the church. Like congregations and broader unions of believers, they seek to demonstrate, represent, and celebrate the new life God gives to the world.

3. All such unions are essential to the reality of the church, in contrast to accidental, arbitrary, or unnecessary. The church cannot exist without being embodied in gatherings of persons for corporate worship, life, and witness, as well as being embodied in forms that unite people throughout the world. There is no mandate for a solitary Christian life, but only for Christians in relation with one another and with non-Christians. Thus we profess that the church

is one, catholic, and ecumenical. It is also apostolic, since we are in relation to the communion of saints in previous ages.

4. All such unions demonstrate, represent, and celebrate the unity of Christ across the barriers of space, class, race, and all other forms of division. They call us out of our localism and extend our life in the church catholic, as well as into the evangelical frontier.

5. Such unions extend the church in relational terms that can and must be inclusive and egalitarian, rather than exclusive and hierarchical. We do not have to imagine or implement such extension in vertical terms, implying a hierarchy of being, with degrees of importance.

6. All ordained ministers hold an office (i.e., an essential role and duty in the life of the church), which includes the witness to this union of believers throughout the world.

   a. On these terms the congregational pastor is a representative of the unity the members have in Christ.

   b. Pastors called to have oversight (an episcopal duty) by means of regional and national offices share in this representation of the reconciliation of Christ. Their office is part of the being of the church, and not simply a function. They are to embody the unity of Christ. Individual members and congregations have an essential need to be united in the church catholic, to receive pastoral care that manifests such a union, and to be inspired by a vision of the worldwide peace of Christ. When regional pastors are defined primarily in terms of functional advantages (i.e., they can do things pastors cannot do), their role is always dependent on the quality and quantity of goods and services. Here we affirm a different relation that abides over time and in the face of disagreement: these pastors are called to represent our unity in Christ.

c. Special agencies and institutions established by the church and/or related to the church must be redefined as offices: they represent an essential element in the church's being, and they are given authority to perform specific duties. As such they are not separate from the church's essential being and mission, to be added on or connected by means of extraordinary measures. Nor are they a hierarchy apart from or above the congregations and governing bodies of the churches. As embodiments of the church's life, they are to be brought into direct relation with the multiple unions of the church (congregational, regional, or national) in ways of responsibility and accountability.

7. Governing bodies for denominations (conferences and synods) represent the unity of congregations, regional bodies, institutions, and agencies within the church. Such gatherings must speak for the church, and not simply to the church, lest they lose their authority. But the right to speak for the church will be granted and supported only if the process is open and inclusive, rather than closed and controlled by special interests. If the process reflects only the culture war, it will further divide the church. But if it represents the new life God gives to the church, it holds within it the hope of liberating and reconciling people now estranged.

Such a reform of the ways we define, organize, and govern the church points to the priority of being over doing. This priority must be affirmed because it is derived from the gospel itself. The being of the church cannot be described simply from a worldly point of view. It is in essence a spiritual community because it has its origin in the presence of God that is transforming the world. Being has priority because God's will to redeem us is prior to all that we do. This implies that only the new being can make possible the proper doing of the church. As the New Testament never tires in affirming, there is the possibility of new practice because of the transformative being of God in Jesus Christ. In this sense, the New Testament is fully aware of the radical description of the human condition, caught in the conflicts of suffering, anger, and violence. Where people are conditioned to accept these powers as the only reality, how can we expect them to act in any other way unless a new reality appears in their realm of experience? If there is an imperative in the New Testament, and of course there is and must be, it is always based on the prior action of God, which creates a new context for our life. As the Johannine theology declares: we love God and our neighbor, because God first loved us.

Agents of Reconciliation:
The Union of Being and Doing

This brings us directly to the relation of being and doing. The church as a divinely created community is a new way of being in the world. It cannot be the people called by God without giving expression to this reality. The reconciliation of God and the world is not first a doctrine, but the reality of the church's life. As Christ was present in time and space only by being faithful in word and deed, so the church must be in time and space, representing the reconciliation of God and the world. It is the nature of the church to participate in this world as did Christ. It is also the nature of the church to witness to reconciliation by bearing and resisting the evil of this world.

If the doing of the Christian life grows naturally and inevitably from the being, then we must conclude that in the church there is an inseparable union of being and doing. In

149

the new being of Jesus Christ, human beings are incorporated into a new, spiritual reality. Conversely, God's action is at work in and through this new reality — including its people and forms. Such a transformation of human action is expressed in numerous places in the New Testament. Compare the Pauline assertion: God is making God's appeal through those called (2 Cor. 5:20). Consider the audacious claim of Jesus that "You are the light of the world" (Matt. 5:14). Or reflect on the Johannine chain of love that extends from God the Father to the Son, then to the disciples and then to the world, that the world might know and love God. But perhaps the most striking example of transformation and empowerment is the great commission of Matthew 28. There Jesus sends the disciples forth to baptize, make disciples, and teach. This is the imperative given to the church. But note that it is not from a distant Lord, but from one who is with them when giving the commission and who promises to be with them until the close of the age. The command is wrapped in a presence and a promise. The church's doing is always taken up into the being of the church, which is the presence of God in Christ, reconciling the world to God.

While we have no difficulty finding agreement in the New Testament on the union of being and doing, such agreement is not always the case today. A variety of alternate ways of relating being and doing come to mind, which only tend to confuse the relation:

1. Doing is something added on to being, like a last point in a sermon that tries to apply the idea. This is especially the case in the individualistic piety of America, where religion is conceived as one's solitary relation to God. That the life of a Christian should of necessity include a confession related to the Apostles' Creed, participation in the communion of the saints, or witness for justice and peace

150

— these are foreign ideas. They are foreign precisely because they were never part of the original agreement, as understood by the believer. Thus the attempt to add them on now, as a call to either doctrinal orthodoxy or moral action, falls on deaf ears.

2. Doing is related to being as the human is related to the divine. In this case, the being of the church is understood as the originating divine presence or power, whereas the doing of the church is understood as the human response. Such a view implies a very mechanical cause/effect relation between God and believers. It also assumes that they are independent agents. This view completely misses the New Testament affirmation of spiritual union between Christ and the believer, as well as the dependence of the believer on God for the empowerment to act.

3. The doing of the church is equated with moral witness and service in the world, in contrast to the being of the gathering church. For activists, doing means works of justice and peace in the world. For an advocate of church renewal such as Kennon Callahan, it means that the mission of the church is defined entirely as action directed toward nonmembers.[1] To be sure, Callahan's position is based on data that support his thesis: effective and growing churches are churches that engage in action directed to those outside the church, and not simply at themselves. But such a definition of mission creates a strange division among the members. Are not those that teach children in the church, visit sick members, sing in the choir, or grow flowers for worship also engaged in the mission (doing) of the church? Why should the church's mission be defined only in terms of activities outside the church? Why

1. Cf. Kennon L. Callahan, *Twelve Keys to an Effective Church: Strategic Planning for Mission* (San Francisco: Harper, 1983), xxviii and 1-10.

is not worship, which is an indispensable act of the church, part of its mission? One is reminded of a declaration from Stanley Hauerwas that worship is the most revolutionary thing Christians can do![2] Like the activist preference for the doing of social witness, Callahan's design creates a hierarchy of activities, and in the end a divided church. If doing refers to all of the activities of our being as Christians, then it ought to include our worship, confession, and fellowship as well as witness and service in the world.

4. If the restriction of doing to certain preeminent actions is divisive, just as divisive is the equation of being with the clergy/church and doing with the laity/world. This split may well be a Protestant version of the medieval orders, though in the latter case it was a distinction between orders of being, with each entailing a specific form of action. In the assignment of doing to laity, the assumption is that they bear the responsibility for taking the gospel into the world, whereas the ministry of the ordained is within the church and to the laity. In certain contexts, this view has a point. William Stringfellow advocated it as a way of undoing the confusion created in the '50s and '60s, when clergy took to the streets because the laity would not claim their baptismal calling.[3] In that situation, Stringfellow argued that clergy needed to recover their ministry of Word and sacrament, whereas laity needed to rediscover witness and service in the world. But like any good idea, it can be overdone. First, the ministry of Word and sacrament is one form of the church's doing; conversely, witness

2. This statement by Stanley Hauerwas came in an address to a pastors' conference in Florida, where I was present.

3. William Stringfellow, *A Private and Public Faith* (Grand Rapids: William B. Eerdmans Publishing Co., 1962), 32-55.

and service in the world is one form of the church's being. Secondly, it simply is too confining to restrict the role of clergy to service within the church and laity to service in the world. We have discovered that there is much to be learned from each office in both places.

If we envision, then, the union of being and doing in the life of the church, what form shall this doing of the church take? Scripture provides multiple enumerations of the church's doing, from the great commission (baptize, make disciples, and teach) to Paul's praise of faith, hope, and love. William Stringfellow expressed it well when he declared that the church is called to discern, rely upon, and celebrate the presence of God in the world.[4] Such a triad, along with numerous other prescriptions, is helpful in pointing the way. Jackson Carroll organizes the life of the church around interpretation, the formation of community, and empowerment of public ministry.[5] As already noted, Kennon Callahan, in his plan for more effective churches, distinguishes between the work internal to the life of the church and the mission directed to those outside the church.

In general, it is best to provide only broad enumerations of what form the church's being in the world should take. To mandate specific action for Christians in radically different times and places contradicts the baptismal calling of every Christian to be faithful where they are. Too often the church has assumed that one group (be it an authoritative body or a protesting group) can set the agenda for everyone. Such practice has inhibited the ability of individual Christians and congregations to discern the implications of the gospel where they

4. Stringfellow, 56.
5. Jackson W. Carroll, *As One with Authority: Reflective Leadership in Ministry* (Louisville: Westminster/John Knox Press, 1991), 99.

are.[6] It has also plunged the church into divisive warfare by the insistence that the church must act collectively on quite specific issues, over which people of goodwill disagree.[7] By contrast, it is preferable to indicate only the most essential requirements for being in the world in a new way:

1. To be reconciled to God and one's neighbor means to confess that this new life is a gift of God. Therefore we cannot keep silent but must engage in the evangelical mandate.
2. To receive such a gift from God evokes worship: acts of repentance, proclamation, and praise. Such worship must be rooted in the reality of Christ's presence (sacraments) and enable us to envision a new world (proclamation).
3. To be reconciled is to be together in community, celebrat-

---

6. A conversation with a pastor illustrates the point. The pastor of a rural congregation indicated that her congregation would not consider the various calls to action from the national offices because they were not applicable or would cause division. When asked to describe her congregation, she indicated that it consisted of large, extended families, which often overlapped. The people seemed to be more interested in issues relating to family life: children, parents, marriage, and home. When I suggested that those issues were most appropriate for the congregation to examine, for the purpose of personal growth and service, the pastor was both enthusiastic and relieved. It was as if she were given permission to set her own agenda, as well as empowered to act in ways faithful to her situation.

7. An example of asking the church to engage in highly specific and complex issues, without proper study, discussion, and prayer, comes from a regional meeting in the United Church of Christ in 1994. The voting delegates were asked to make specific recommendations to the national government on the withdrawal of the embargo against Cuba, imposition of an embargo against China, and policies toward Latin America. The problem here is not that the church seeks to speak to the powers of the world. The problem is in the level of specificity, as well as the process of asking several hundred delegates to formulate a policy guided by parliamentary rules of order, where one must vote yes or no.

ing the presence of God's gift and growing together in Christ.

4. To be reconciled is to engage in the work of reconciliation: to share the good news, to practice the forgiveness of wrongs done against us, to resist the powers of evil, and to be agents of reconciliation.
5. To be reconciled is to pray and hope for the reconciliation of all people and things according to the divine will.
6. In all of these forms of action, it must be remembered that the first act of a Christian is to be. It is to represent in one's life the integrity of faith, hope, and love in the face of pretense and divided loyalties, despair, and anger.

The New Humanity

If this enumeration represents essential marks of a new way of being in the world, but not an exhaustive list, can it be used to contrast the being and doing of Christians in the face of alternate forms of life? Can these marks be tested by how they relate to the problems and issues that threaten the identity of the church? Here it is appropriate to recall that in Chapter One we argued that the message of the gospel is undercut by individualism and functionalism. In Chapter Three we named alternative ways we are moved to define our identity and worth: independence and differentiation, suffering and victimization, anger, and finally ideological claims. How does the gospel of reconciliation, as embodied in the being and doing of the church, speak to these issues?

The answer to these questions may be introduced by recounting a conversation with a friend regarding this essay. As I was engaged in the preliminary organizing of the material, my friend asked about the subject. When I responded that it dealt with being liberated from the ideological warfare of our day and living without the claims that lead to so much division, my friend replied, "It sounds like you are asking for a change in human nature." His reply reduced me to silence. To admit his point opened the possibility that this essay would be an exercise in idealistic dreaming — a project people smile at, but quickly pass by. To deny it would be just as alarming, since that is precisely what is needed. Having reflected on the question as the essay developed, I really have no answer but to admit that such a change is what is announced in the gospel. A transformation is involved, not in our genetic coding, but in the way we define our identity and worth, in our being and doing, in the way we perceive what is ultimate acting on us and in the way we act on other people and the world.

Our analysis of our cultural situation and our reading of the gospel share a basic assumption: that we are acculturated into an environment of habits and traditions, beliefs and values, and claims — both modest and ultimate — about ourselves, our family, and society. What we have described in the first three chapters is the way we perceive the environment given to us by religion in America. Conversely, the history of Israel and the announcement by Jesus of the coming of God's Rule represent the creation of a counterenvironment or realm of experience. What Jesus says and does, and especially how he responds to the forces about him, constitute his demonstration of a new way of being and doing in the very world that wills to destroy him. He invites persons who participate fully in the first world to enter a new and second world, which he calls the Rule of God. Some are ordinary people, others have authority, some live in disgrace and feel cut off, still others have accepted their status as victims. To this mixed audience Jesus displays power to overcome the forces of that first world: he heals the sick, forgives sins, shares food with outcasts, befriends women and children, cleanses the temple, interprets the Scriptures in new ways. In countless ways Jesus opens the eyes of his listeners to see the providential care of God at work in the world, but overlooked in their preoccupation with the first world's agenda. In effect, Jesus changes the context for human life and therefore redefines who we are and what is possible. His commission to the disciples to live in a new way, to baptize, to make disciples, and to teach would not make sense if he had not said earlier: "'Go and tell John what you have seen and heard: the blind receive their sight, the lame walk, the lepers are cleansed, the deaf hear, the dead are raised, the poor have good news brought to them'" (Luke 7:30 NRSV).

Paul, as an interpreter of Jesus, understands full well that Jesus means a divine intervention that changes the conditions for human existence. Cross and resurrection mean that the old world is passing away and a new world is dawning. Paul speaks of an old self and a new self, old ways of thinking and the new mind of Christ, life according to the divisions (claims) of the world versus the new humanity created in Christ. While Paul's vocabulary is quite different from that of the Synoptic Gospels or John, the essential message is the same: Jesus Christ means change and new possibilities.

We are suggesting that the being and doing of Christians are made possible by the transformative power of God revealed in the gospel. Such an experience is analogous to a variety of experiences in which we are transformed by events. For example, there is the experience of being loved, which overcomes fear and self-doubt, and opens up a new horizon of possibilities. Being loved changes the self and makes it possible to risk action otherwise deemed unrealistic. In a similar way the birth of a child generates joy and wonder (as well as fear) far beyond our expectations. Many speak of the beauty of sunrise or sunset, the quiet of the forest or the grandeur of mountains, which overwhelm and evoke a response. Within our social history we have numerous instances where we are transformed by a common experience. The American experience of pluralism has generated broad forms of unity in the face of formidable barriers. While we have never achieved the goals of equality and freedom for all, the fact is that in America most people have learned to live non-violently amid radical difference. Protestants, Catholics, and Jews have forged a consensus that represents a noble achievement.

We can also point to the way bonds of community have been created through the shedding of blood. Every war has left the survivors remembering the sacrifice of patriots. Lincoln memorialized the courage and sacrifice of the dead at Gettysburg, connecting their death to the values on which the nation rested. The listeners were thereby obligated, according to Lincoln, to participate in the struggle to preserve freedom and the union. The fiftieth anniversary of the Normandy invasion in World War II also illustrated the power of events to transform persons in ways far beyond their own action. In countless testimonies, veterans of that war and other wars confess that the experience of warfare changed forever their lives and bound them to their companions. The power of bloodshed to bind people together was clearly demonstrated in the assassinations of John F. Kennedy and Martin Luther King, Jr. In the one case, people still compare notes on what they were doing when they heard the news of the death of the president. In the other case, the death of an innocent and noble witness prompted many to see the evils present in racism. Finally, we can refer again to the peace agreement between Israel and the PLO, signed in September 1993. In an effort to explain what brought them to the agreement, Prime Minister Rabin said: "We the soldiers who have returned from the battle stained with blood, we who have fought against you, the Palestinians, we say to you in a loud and clear voice: Enough of blood and tears! Enough!"[8]

These examples illustrate that people can be transformed by events and find themselves acting in new ways, even ways

8. *New York Times,* September 14, 1993, p. A1.

contrary to their own expectations. They find that they are bound together by something that has happened to them. Their lives are changed with respect to their identity and they are enabled, even required, to act in new ways. Such examples can assist us in understanding the gospel, whereby the cross transforms the way people think about themselves and what they consider possible in this world. It should not surprise us that Paul must develop, as we noted earlier, a new vocabulary for understanding the transformative power of the gospel (e.g., the tension between the old and new self, as well as the awareness that we no longer live unto ourselves but live in Christ or in the Spirit). This vocabulary points to the radical change generated by the gospel. And, of course, there is the wonder-filled reference to going out of our minds:

> For if we are beside ourselves, it is for God; if we are in our right mind, it is for you. For the love of Christ urges us on, because we are convinced that one has died for all; therefore all have died. And he died for all, so that those who live might live no longer for themselves, but for him who died and was raised for them. (2 Cor. 5:13-15 NRSV)

> If then there is any encouragement in Christ, any consolation from love, any sharing in the Spirit, any compassion and sympathy, make my joy complete: be of the same mind, having the same love, being in full accord and of one mind. Do nothing from selfish ambition or conceit, but in humility regard others as better than yourselves. Let each of you look not to your own interests, but to the interests of others. Let the same mind be in you that was in Christ Jesus. (Phil. 2:1-5 NRSV)

From this perspective the church can and must speak directly to the signs of our time that govern the way we view the world and ourselves.

1. The gospel of reconciliation declares that identity and worth are gifts of God to each person, that each person is valued and claimed by God. Such a gift is not dependent on the approval of family, friends, or the state. The church must always stand with those whose identity is denied and against the forces that dehumanize persons because of who they are. Grace means that every person is created by God and loved eternally. Grace also means that persons find their identity in community, be it the circles of family, friendship, or faith. The unity of Christian community is not the loss of individual identity, but the way individuals come to understand themselves as brothers and sisters in Christ.

2. To participate in life, as did Christ, is to suffer. The community of Christ must acknowledge the multiple ways people suffer and take them into its life. In so doing it must stand against the conspiracy of silence regarding serious illness and the pain of death. It must also name many of the sufferings for what they are, namely, pain that is self-inflicted or caused by broad patterns in our society. But in the face of all of this suffering, the community of Christ must resist the temptation to be defined by illness and death, or to respond by inflicting more suffering and death on ourselves or others. In the face of so much suffering, which at times is unbearable and which we cannot control, the community of Christ must practice patience, trust, and hope in God. There are times when we have no response but to affirm that we believe in the resurrection of the dead.

3. The way of Christ, which is the way of reconciliation, must also confront the overwhelming presence of anger and violence in our society. We must name them for what they are: the powers of death. The gospel declares that Christ bore the hostility of the world, indeed, that this is in truth

God bearing rejection by the world. Our hope is in the God who breaks the cycle of anger by overcoming it with justice and love, mercy and goodness. There can be no alternative to the cycle of anger and violence in the Christian community unless it takes up the practice of forgiving one another for wrongs done.

4. Against the ideology of the world, wherein we make ourselves and our future by our claims, Christians are called to live without ultimate claims but one, namely, the grace of God. Such defenselessness is possible because we are claimed by God in Christ. It also authorizes the ministry of reconciliation. The community of Christ is called to stand against and between conflicting claims that would condemn opponents to disgrace or death. It must bear the burden of condemnation for not joining every specific dispute. It must insist that both parties are responsible to God and that there is usually a third way. Above all, it must witness to the new basis of union God gives, wherein we might find nonviolent ways of living together.

Naming Those Who Are Called

The redefinition of the church advocated here points to the importance of language. One need only consider that the name given to the new community of reconciliation (i.e., the church) means literally "those who are called." Here is a name that gives expression to its unusual reality and purpose, irrevocably tied to a sequence of events. When the names for the church are filled with wonder, they catch our imagination and open before us a new world of possibilities. At the same time, wrongly chosen words confine our imaginations and limit possibilities. For example, the concept of voluntary association as a definition of the church confines our thinking to the horizontal reality of human decision making. While the concept serves well to emphasize that membership in the church involves a free decision, it fails to lift before us the fact that the church is grounded in God's goodwill, which creates a new spiritual reality in this world.

The importance of the language used to name the church is underscored by the simple fact that the early Christians were forced to find a new language to express the reality of what was happening to them in Jesus Christ. The dominant images for the church give expression to the reconciliation of God and humanity as a new spiritual life now present in the world. Consider the images of the *Body of Christ* in Paul and the *vine and branches* in the Gospel of John. We note immediately that both are organic metaphors, rather than images drawn from social organization or legal contracts. As living organisms, they open a new way of understanding the relation of the believer and God, as well as the relation between believers. This point cannot be overemphasized, especially in the rejection of mechanistic images, wherein independent agents seek to affect one another by means of cause and effect. Neither the Pauline nor the Johannine image allows us to understand what happens in Christ in a mechanical way, that is, God acts, humans react, God responds, and so on. In both Paul and John the organic images focus on the unity of the believer with God in Christ. It is a spiritual unity of new life, not an exchange of goods or a contract. It is certainly not like the tentative commitment that is implied today when lovers claim to have a *relationship*.

These two images also emphasize the radical change involved in becoming a Christian. One is no longer the same person: John tells the story of Nicodemus being born again; Paul speaks of dying and rising (Rom. 6), going out of one's mind (2 Cor. 5:13), and having a new mind, the mind of Christ (Phil. 2). In the Pauline image of the body, the change involves a unity of diverse members under the Lordship of Christ. The image of the body allows Paul to deal with the dialectic of unity and plurality without destroying either. It also allows for a strong recognition of the dependence of each member on Christ as Lord as well as the other members. Because the members are different, each is valued and contributes to the life of the other. Unity happens not in spite of their differences but in and through them. By contrast, the image of the vine and branches does not illustrate as well the dynamic of unity and plurality, since all branches are the same and have the same relation to the vine. Nor does it emphasize as much the mutual dependence of the members: one branch could be removed from the vine with far less stress than the loss of an arm or eye to the body. But what the vine/branches image does do in the most radical way is emphasize the life-giving relationship of all believers with Christ. Here is a spiritual relation that creates, sustains, and nourishes believers. John develops this dependence in two ways: on the one hand their continued life is completely dependent on their connection with Christ. To be severed from Christ would be an end to the new life. But the same consequence would occur if a member were to choose to be a Christian apart from Christ. There is no new birth apart from Christ. On the other hand, their ability to act (i.e., bear fruit) also depends on their relation with Christ. Here we see that the use of vine and branches in John corresponds to the image of the good tree in the Synoptic Gospels. Good fruit comes only from a good tree. One cannot get good fruit from a bad tree, nor can one get it by working with the branches. The good tree is the source of the good fruit; the new being precedes the new doing. Those working to change the action of Christians by means other than spiritual renewal need to take note. The church cannot be changed by anything less than the transformative power of the gospel. John, however, does not leave it there. Branches that bear no fruit are cut off! The fruit of the vine analogy is thus used twice: once to emphasize that branches can bear fruit only if connected to the vine, then again to underscore the imperative that branches must bear fruit. John thus affirms the priority of being over doing and the union of being and doing. In one image John gives the church a defense against boasting born of self-reliance and a warning against inaction.

The organic images of Body of Christ and vine and branches cannot be surpassed in terms of their ability to convey essential points about the church: (1) Membership involves a transformative experience whereby the old way of life ceases and a new way begins. It is a new spiritual life of radical dependence on God in Christ, in contrast to the independence of the old life, based on the standards of the world. (2) To be a part of this new spiritual life is to be united with other members in mutual dependence. (3) The church is a gift from God; it is something we receive and do not create. Whenever we need to confess and/or insist on these points, the Johannine and Pauline images are authoritative. These two images are limited, however, precisely because they are organic analogies, that is, they compare a community of people confessing faith in Jesus Christ to living organisms. But since the church is not in actuality vine and branches, or a physical body, it will be helpful to ask, are there other images to convey the reconciliation of God with the world? Are there images drawn from the experience of human communities that can be used to understand the new life of reconciliation found in Jesus Christ?

Such images will need to give expression to the characteristics just named: transformative power, being united in the face of division, and receiving a gift. If we accept these as standards, then two popular categories will have limited use. One is the image of the family, where people are bound together by blood. This has limits since those gathered together in congregations are usually not blood relatives. Moreover, we are looking for images that create unity among those not naturally bound together. In the face of multiple divisions based on blood and ethnic background, people need confidence that there can be unity on grounds other than family status. The second image of limited use is a legal contract. In a multitude of ways we bind ourselves to others through bills of sale, contracts, terms of employment, memberships, and financial pledges. But while the legal models are prevalent, and may dominate our lives, they move us away from the experience of the gospel. Legal contracts are self-initiated. They involve mutual agreement based on voluntary consent, which can be withdrawn. We have argued that one of the ailments afflicting the American church is precisely the mind-set that the church is one more voluntary association, which human beings create, maintain, or dissolve. Even more to the point, the legal agreements are between members. They do not allow for understanding the way the members are substantively changed, the commingling of life and the introduction of a new form of life through the intervention of God.

The New Testament contains an image of the church not yet mentioned, which connects with general human experience, that may well be appropriate for our time. It is the image of the *household of God* in Ephesians 2:19. Remember that this image of the transformative power of God comes at the conclusion of the declaration of peace through the cross of Jesus. In Christ, God has broken down the dividing wall of hostility between conflicted groups. Peace means a new basis of union between Jew and Gentile, men and women, rich and poor, persons divided by race and national origin. The designations of enemy, stranger, and sojourner have been replaced by that of fellow citizen. Such a change does not automatically imply that all of the tensions and points of disagreement have been overcome. Nor does it erase the memory of old wounds. What it does suggest is that enemies, strangers, and sojourners are brought together into a new place that has boundaries and structure: it is the household of God. Within this place, old ways of dealing with one another are set aside — by God's command and the human recognition that they are destructive. Within this place, people are given new names and new identities: they are fellow citizens. This new self-understanding or identity by virtue of God's transforming power leads to the mandate "to lead a life worthy of the calling to which you have been called" (Eph. 4:1). This peace is within a framework — the household of God — which is built on "the foundation of the apostles and prophets, Christ Jesus himself being the chief cornerstone" (Eph. 2:20). The image of the household of God witnesses both to the priority of divine presence in creating a new place and to the union of being and doing.

Consider how the image of a household, understood as God's new creation, opens up ways for understanding the being and doing of the church:

- In God's household there are many rooms, enough for everyone in spite of their number and differences, to live in peace.
- In a household people are known by name.
- As in most households, the sharing of food is the means of sustenance, unity, and fellowship.
- Households must care for children and honor older persons.
- As in all households, its members suffer and must deal with death and grief.
- There is diversity, disagreement, and conflict within the framework set by the unity of the household.
- It is a refuge and safe house, where one can always find entrance.
- There is music to celebrate life's joys and sorrows, and, above all, to praise God.

Is it too much to ask for the church to be the household of God? Such a move would begin with the recognition that the church is the gift of God and not our creation. Like the medieval cathedrals, the household of God would be formed by the cross of Christ, reminding us that we come to this safe house only by the suffering of the Son of God. In this place, where the Word is proclaimed and bread and wine are shared, those who are opposite and different, even enemies, could gather to receive the peace of Christ. And just as cathedrals were built to be seen by all for miles around as a witness to the presence of peace on earth, so the household of God would be present in the world as a witness to reconciliation. Such churches would take up the way of Christ in the face of, in between, and against the competing ideologies of our day: bearing the hostility of the world, resisting evil by means of good, and always praying and hoping for the coming of God's Rule.

The Household of God: Images of Reconciliation

Our assessment of the current situation suggests that we need broad images of the church that are inclusive rather than exclusive, liberating rather than oppressive. They need to point to the fact that the church belongs to God. Even more important, they must witness to the fact that the church is both a place where reconciliation exists, in which we can live and be at peace, and a process, in which we grow by grace into the final unity of Christ. The concept *household of God* may possess these characteristics, providing us with glimpses of the new being here on earth. In this last section of this essay we shall suggest how the church, understood as God's household, might be more inclusive. In such a way the church might point to the wonder and joy of reconciling grace. It should be noted that the ability to approach old divisions with an irenic inclusiveness is directly related to the view of the work of Christ: in him God has united all things.

Reconsidering the Eight Images of the Church

In Chapter Two we developed a typology regarding the nature of the church, suggesting that all eight types represented positive elements that belong to the essence of the church. We also declined to develop a formula whereby they might all fit together, since our task is not to produce a theory, but to develop actual churches that are more inclusive. What we can do is affirm that all eight are compatible and point to the fullness of the church. Since God's household has many rooms, where people of many traditions and practices are invited to live together in the peace of Christ, it is appropriate to consider how each type brings a gift to the table of the Lord.

Of the eight types discussed, four make statements about the being of the church: Sacramental Participation in the Historic Community, Confessing the True Faith, Rebirth in the Spirit, and the Pilgrim Church. The first points to the transformative power of Christ in sacraments and community. The second affirms the centrality of the gospel, as a word of judgment as well as of grace. The third insists that sacrament, community, or proclamation has no power without the life-giving Spirit. It is pointless to argue about the preeminence of any one of these on biblical or theological grounds. In the household of God all are present. But we have added another to this group (i.e., Pilgrim) dealing with the being of the church. When taken in its positive form, the Pilgrim image is concerned about the being of the church, rather than the relation of being and doing. Unlike the three just mentioned, however, the Pilgrim image is more of a prophetic warning and affirmation of the sovereignty of God. It is a reminder that we not become so involved in our statements about sacraments and church, proclamation and rebirth, that we absolutize them and convert the life-giving gospel into a tool of repression. Pilgrims have always left their homes because they did not find there the paradise their neighbors claimed. In the household of God, there is room for those who are still seeking the answer and who caution us against turning our claims into ideology.

There is considerable tension between these four images of the being of the church, which ultimately points to the tensions present within the being of the church itself. One way of exposing this tension is to explore the polarity between *participation/belonging* and *confession born of persuasion*. That is to say, the life of the church alternates between being and affirming, celebrating what is and reminding itself why it is. Participation/belonging has its symbols and even organizational forms, all based on being members, bound together in the Body of Christ. Members participate by habit and/or loyalty. They have internalized the rationale for action, and they understand the connection between privilege and responsibility. By contrast, confession born of persuasion asks at the beginning, but again and again, why should I believe and what should I do? It focuses on the decision of joining; its medium is persuasion. In its most elementary form, joining even asks questions that the members consider to be rude: "Why should I give?" or "Why should I obligate myself?" One way of looking at the decline of the Protestant mainline is to see it as the result of an overreliance on participation/belonging. Whether it relied too self-confidently on the proper administration of the sacrament, or sound doctrine, or the once-given Spirit, or answers given long ago, in each case it assumed that belonging eliminated persuasion. It thought that all it had to do was celebrate the community of faith, that it could forget about the persuasion directed toward its children and society. The wonder-filled celebration of the sacraments and the proclamation of the Word were focused on participation rather than persuasion, celebrating rather than reminding. In such a situation the activist churches provided no help: they assumed that all we needed to do was admonish the members, and they sacrificed education, which is the community's process of persuasion. They forgot that we are at one and the same time justified and sinful, being and becoming Christian. For both those inside and those outside the church, the loss of persuasion has allowed the celebration of belonging to lose its driving force.

The tension between belonging and persuasion is present in each of these four images of the church, though in radically different ways. Roman Catholics might apply this analysis to their own tradition, which has depended so heavily on the celebration of sacramental participation rather than persuasion. In theory, Protestants of the Right Faith type should be strong on persuasion, but history reveals multiple ways in which they overrely on belonging: state churches, unofficial establishments, and alignments with culture. The conversion of the gospel into absolutely correct doctrine and/or an infallible Bible has meant the loss of persuasion: there are no more questions; the lively debate is reduced to silence. Faith has been changed from living without claims and trusting in God alone to belonging to an authoritative community that has absolute knowledge. Those claiming rebirth in the Spirit are also not immune to the loss of the tension. The Anabaptist, Baptist, and Pentecostal traditions have known the problems of doctrinal and legal rigidity. Pilgrims and Seekers, on the other hand, may have so absolutized their search that they are unable to experience the full celebration of participation and belonging.

Perhaps one doorway into a new living arrangement between these four images of the church would be to explore how participation/belonging and persuasion are present in our traditions. If these two sides of our life are polar elements, intrinsic to living communities, then we need to own them and explore ways to affirm them.

The remaining four images of the church in our typology can be grouped together because they make statements about how being and doing are united. These four types are Acts of Love and Justice, World Unity, the Covenant Community, and the Solidarity of Jesus with Those Who Suffer. All four point to where Christ is present in the world: Christ is present in deeds of love and justice, in the reconciliation of all peoples, in the gathering of covenant communities, and in solidarity with those who suffer. Who can argue against any one of these as an appropriate answer to the question of Christ's presence? To be sure, one or more of these affirmations have been misused in particular cases, but that can be said of every image of the church. But in God's household, all of these have a place at the table of the Lord, for Christ has promised to be with us in each of the places named in these four types.

While these four images differ in their answer to how Christ is present in the world, they stand united in raising a challenge to the previous set of four. This has to do with the age-old relation of justification and sanctification. How does the affirmation of the radical gift of unconditional grace relate to the call to become what is promised? Mainline Protestantism has been myopic on this issue. It has been so terrified of the excesses of revivalism, the rigidity of perfectionist movements, and the illusions of utopianism that it has settled into complacency. So convinced that the Rule of God will not come through such schemes and programs, it is nearly speechless regarding the possibilities of change for the individual or society. It reduces the gospel to an eschatological stalemate: God may be gracious, but God does not expect much of us and we cannot expect much of God. Content with a religion of grace, it provides comfort and assurance. What is thereby ignored is the religion of power, which speaks the language of hope for

171

change, built on the fact that God is present and is in the process of changing things.[9]

The four images in this last set share a passion for sanctification: they radiate confidence that God is changing us and the world. They differ as to the focus of that change, and those differences are important for the life of the church. Each points to an essential way we are to grow: in acts of love and justice, in gathered communities as well as in unity with other Christians, and in solidarity with those who suffer. There are obviously other ways to speak of growing into the fullness of Christ. Together they remind those images dealing so strongly with the being of the church that the church is always the community called to become more fully the people of God.

What we have then is not a formula, a chart, or three easy steps on how to incorporate all eight into a congregation. Rather, we have a word of praise for the richness of the church in its many forms, each a glimpse of reconciliation. Our task is to wonder in word and deed how we might make our congregations and denominations as inclusive as the household of God.

9. In analyzing the tensions between the so-called mainline Protestant churches and the Free Church traditions associated with revivalism and Pentecostalism, it is helpful to distinguish between grace and power. The religion of grace focuses on God's acceptance of sinners by unconditional love; the religion of power focuses on how God is changing things now. The former affirms the sovereignty of God against tyrannical powers, but is very cautious about utopian schemes. It also tends to be horrified at the excessive promises made by the religion of power, which appear to be attempts to manipulate both believers and God. By contrast, the religion of power expects something of God and vigorously declares that God expects something of us — now! There are obviously high correlations between the religion of power and the powerless. The religion of power tends to see its counterpart as far too comfortable and allied with the status quo. To determine which type is present in one's own tradition, simply note the dominant images in the worship and/or sermon: do they have to do with grace and love or change and expectation?

Reorganizing Congregations

Another example of the inclusivity of the household of God relates to the organizational forms of churches in America. By and large, they fall into the three categories of *parish, congregation,* and *movement.*

A parish is a church that has definite geographical boundaries and takes as its special mission the ministry to people in that space. While the idea of parish may have originated in the context of a state church, where space is literally divided up, it still exists in many denominations in America. It could be a neighborhood or section of a city. Small-town churches are often parishes by default, since the town streets come to an end at the edge of farmland or forest, and the people in the town and nearby country constitute the known world for the church. The key to the parish is the linkage between the church and the people/land in this place. The church does not move if people move; it endures changes in membership, economy, and society. If radical shifts occur in race and class, a parish still stands as the church for people in this place, because it defines ministry as the care of people in this place. For a parish, the question is, how can we be faithful to Christ in this place?

By contrast, congregations are covenant communities that gather for worship, education, fellowship, and service. They are primarily communities of discipleship, seeking to grow together in faith and love. Since the congregation is organized around participation in discipleship, the congregation need not be bound to a particular place. Congregations can move. Their members can move but still belong, often commuting great distances because of the bonds of fellowship. New members tend to be drawn not necessarily from the neighborhood of the church, but from people who wish to join such a community. Thus congregations tend to be fairly homogeneous with respect to race, class, and ethnic background. Congregations can also

173

exist at an original site without much contact with the immediate neighborhood, precisely because they are not parishes. Ministry in a congregation will be defined in terms of nurturing and strengthening the community of disciples. For a congregation, the question is, how can we grow as disciples of Christ?

The third form, which we call a movement, defines the church in terms of special witness and service. It will concede that a building may be needed, but has little interest in the church as an institution with physical property, organization, rules and procedures, and programs. It tends to prefer spontaneity to structure, action to contemplation. For a movement, the question is, what is God doing in the world? This concern for discerning the presence of the Spirit in new ways causes a movement to spend time listening with care to what is happening in the world and developing strategies for appropriate responses.

The three forms suggest three distinct organizing principles for churches. Most Protestant churches are congregations, not bound by parish lines but concerned about being communities of discipleship. Some are parishes, and some may be a combination of congregation/parish. There are probably fewer movement churches, though there are members and pastors in parishes and congregations who identity with this third form. The distinction allows us to understand how local churches differ in their ethos and sense of mission. But it also allows us to understand some of the conflict internal to a particular church. For example, if a church that is clearly a *congregation* hires a pastor who believes strongly in the *parish* or *movement* form, what will happen? If great care is not taken in resolving the differences, that church will probably be hiring a new pastor very soon. By contrast, the reverse is also a prescription for conflict: a pastor defining ministry in terms of *congregation* will probably not understand the expectations of a *parish*. Since there are probably more pastors than churches that define themselves by the form of *movement,* how will such pastors fare in parishes and congregations? This will become more and more an issue as a new generation of pastors comes to ministry with a liberation theology perspective.

The analysis can also be used to understand the tensions among the members of a local church. Every local church has members who identify with each of the three forms. Depending on the specific denomination and local history, the members will probably identify with parish or congregation. Those identifying with the church as movement are usually ignored or tolerated, and are usually prevented from exercising major influence. But they are present and raise movement questions. Such questions fly in the face of discussions about the budget, a new wing for the church, or general programs (unless the discussion has to do with introducing contemporary social issues into the Sunday School curriculum). The same is true of members representing the parish and congregation types, when they are in the minority. Concerns for the parish focus on the care of people in this place. When a parish concern joins with a movement interest, one might find issues regarding the care of the earth — if the issues are in this parish. Concerns for the community of discipleship might move in the direction of growth of membership or growth of the spiritual life. Such concerns easily connect with evangelism overseas — often avoiding evangelism in the neighborhood of the church.

One cannot work with this threefold schema too long before connections between the three forms and the doctrine of the Trinity emerge. In one sense, the parish is given to us by "God the Father Almighty, maker of heaven and earth." By contrast, congregations focus on the Word incarnate in Jesus Christ and the commission Christ gives, be it the service of love or the evangelical mandate to make disciples. Movements are Spirit-filled organizations, enthused and guided by the Holy Spirit. If we can recognize that the creative power of each of the three organizational forms comes from the richness in God, perhaps we might become more tolerant of the variety between and within our churches. Most of the time we have been quite singularly minded, closed to an alternate organizing principle. We have allowed churches to be polarized and divided over whether money should be spent locally or abroad, whether our mission is to fix up the building, expand the educational program, or fund acts of love and justice. What would happen if a local church elected to reorganize and incorporate all three forms into its life: a concern for the community where the church is; growth in discipleship; and public witness and service in the world? What if the governing body were divided into three committees, with each given one of these tasks? Such a transformation might be an image of reconciliation. In the household of God, there is room for all three, because in God the Father, Son, and Holy Spirit are one.

Index of Names and Subjects